MAKE YOUR TEAM A WINNER!
IDEAS AND INSIGHTS
FOR DEVELOPING TEAM SKILLS

Illustration by Dave Calver

DARTNELL is a publisher serving the world of business with books, manuals, newsletters and bulletins, and training materials for executives, managers, supervisors, salespeople, financial officers, personnel executives, and office employees. Dartnell also produces management and sales training videos and audiocassettes, publishes many useful business forms, and many of its materials and films are available in languages other than English. Dartnell, established in 1917, serves the world's business community. For details, catalogs, and product information write:

THE DARTNELL CORPORATION
4660 N. Ravenswood Avenue
Chicago, IL 60640-4595, U.S.A.
Or phone (800) 621-5463 in U.S. and Canada
www.dartnellcorp.com

Except where noted, this book may not be reproduced, stored in a retrieval system, or transmitted in whole or in part in any form or by any means (electronic, mechanical, photocopying, recording, or otherwise) without prior written permission of The Dartnell Corporation, 4660 N. Ravenswood Avenue, Chicago, IL 60640-4595.

This publication is designed to provide accurate and authoritative information in regard to the subject matter covered. It is sold with the understanding that the publisher is not engaged in rendering legal, accounting, or other professional service. If legal advice or other expert assistance is required, the services of a competent professional person should be sought.
— *From a Declaration of Principles jointly adopted by a Committee of the American Bar Association and a Committee of Publishers.*

Copyright 1998 in the United States, Canada, and Britain by
THE DARTNELL CORPORATION

ISBN #0-85013-341-6
Library of Congress #98-073593

Contents

Introduction xi

1. Learning the Value of Teamwork 1
    Proving Teamwork Works 2
    Exercise: Lost on the Moon 3
    Getting Off to a Good Start 6
    Tip: Friendly Exchanges 8
    Understanding Your Mission 8
    Take a Moment to ...
        Write a Mission Statement 9
    Making Resolutions 10
    Take a Moment to ...
        Clarify Ground Rules 11
    Setting Goals 12
    Take a Moment to ...
        Formulate a Plan 13
    Staying on Track 14
    Exercise: Test Your Team's Commitment 15
    What Would You Do? 16
    Team Activity 16

2. Building a Strong Team 17
    Generating Positive Team Spirit 18
    Take a Moment to ...
        Do Some Cheerleading 19

Tip: Field Trips 20
Exercise: Assess Your Cohesiveness 21
Improving Team Communication 22
Exercise: Start Talking 23
Maintaining Team Focus 24
Finding Power as a Team 25
Determining Your Success 26
Exercise: Evaluate Your Team 27
What Would You Do? 28
Team Activity 28

3. Becoming a Better Team Leader 29

Learning Leadership Skills 30

Take a Moment to ...
    Make a Team Leader Wish List 33

Exercise: Test Your Leadership Potential 34
Meeting Tips for Team Leaders 35
Sparking Team Creativity 36
Tip: Get Help to Meet Deadlines 38
Avoiding Team Roadblocks 39
Exercise: Improve Your Leadership Effectiveness ...41
What Would You Do? 42
Team Activity 42

4. Being a Better Team Member 43

Performing Up to Par 44

Exercise: Are You a Responsible Team Member? 45

Helping Teammates Improve Performance 46

Handling Diversity 48

Take a Moment to ...
    Find Common Ground 49

Tip: Good News 50

Exercise: Do You Work Effectively on a Team? 51

What Would You Do? 52

Team Activity 52

5. Understanding Team Dynamics 53

Seeing the Pieces of the Puzzle 54

Take a Moment to ...
    Look at Roles Within Your Team 56

Determining Your Team's Personality 57

Take a Moment to ...
    Assess Your Team's Personality 58

Understanding Group Communication 59

Exercise: What's Your Style? 61

Tip: The Right Signals 64

Speaking the Team Language 65

Welcoming New Members 66

Tip: Roll Out the Welcome Mat 67

Exercise: Do You Follow the Code? 68

What Would You Do? 69

Team Activity 69

6. Improving Team Meetings 71

Building a Better Meeting 72

Take a Moment to ...
Find Ways to Combat Meeting Apathy 74

Finding a Facilitator 75

Tip: Meeting Agenda 77

Take a Moment to ...
Judge Your Meetings 78

Bringing Meetings Under Control 78

Tip: Chat Time 78

The Meeting Overrunneth 79

Tip: Dog Days 80

Exercise: Beat Meeting Deadlock 81

Using Audiovisual Aids 82

Take a Moment to ...
Create a Colorful Slide Presentation 83

Exercise: Get More Out of Team Meetings 84

What Would You Do? 85

Team Activity 85

7. Coping with Conflict 87

Understanding Conflict 88

Take a Moment to ...
　Decide How Important It Is to Win 90

Watching Out for Hidden Agendas 91

Dealing with Difficult People 92

Tip: The Team Grouch 94

Exercise: Are *You* a Difficult Person? 95

Finding Common Ground When a
　Co-worker Doesn't Like You 96

Resolving Arguments Among Team Members 97

Tip: My Regrets 98

Learning to Laugh 99

Exercise: How Well Does Your Team
　Resolve Conflict? 100

What Would You Do? 102

Team Activity 102

8. Problem-Solving 103

Searching for Solutions 104

Tip: Three Steps to Problem-Solving 104

Brainstorming 105

Thinking Creatively 107

Tip: The Dream Team 108

Take a Moment to ...
　Get Your Creative Juices Flowing 109

Exercise: Choose the Best Solution 109

Understanding Problems 111

Finding Solutions ... Fast! 112

Take a Moment to ...
    Get Unstuck 113

Calling In an Expert 114

Exercise: Improving Skills in Problem-Solving 115

What Would You Do? 116

Team Activity 116

9. A Team Member's Guide to Personal Development and Well-Being 117

Finding Success 118

Take a Moment to ...
    Fine-Tune Your Conversation Skills 121

Tip: Office Language 122

Staying Challenged 122

Managing Time 123

Tip: Double Duty 125

Tip: Time Misspent 127

Take a Moment to ...
    Clean Your Desk 127

Exercise: You *Can* Be More Organized! 129

Managing Stress 130

Tip: Tune Out 131

Tip: Weekend Respite 132

Take a Moment to ...
    Exercise While You Work..132

Tip: Rest Your Eyes..133

Exercise: Check Your Health...134

Making the Most of a Bad Day 135

Battling Burnout..136

Celebrating Success..137

Take a Moment to ...
    Have a Party...137

Exercise: Do You Have a Winning Attitude?......................138

What Would You Do? 139

Team Activity..139

Conclusion...141

INTRODUCTION

If there's one term that sums up the nature of doing business at the turn of the century, it's teamwork. The old hierarchical pyramid is being abandoned in favor of the more creative circle. For workers at all levels, there is more opportunity to contribute — and more responsibility.

You already may be part of a formal team working on a specific project. Or you may be part of a work group — a traditional department made up of people who serve different functions but depend on one another. Either way, knowing how to be a team player will be an important factor in your success.

Unfortunately, however, team skills are not necessarily inborn.

Walk around a grade-school playground and you'll see that, while some children seem to have a natural sense of camaraderie, others are better described as loners. And these loner children eventually grow up, find their way into the workforce ... and cringe at the thought of working in a team setting.

That's where *MAKE YOUR TEAM A WINNER!* comes in. Whether you are a natural team player, a born leader — or a born loner — the tips and exercises offered in the following chapters can help you become a better team member.

You'll discover there are a variety of factors that influence team success. And you'll learn proven methods of team-building.

This book will also help you understand the dynamics of team interaction and provide tips for resolving team conflicts, spicing up meetings, and solving problems. Finally, *MAKE YOUR TEAM A WINNER!* will focus on your personal development, with advice on such topics as coping with stress and managing time.

MAKE YOUR TEAM A WINNER!

So, take some time to read through the suggestions offered here and to complete the exercises. With a little work, you could help your team become more productive and successful — and you could become a most valuable player.

MAKE YOUR TEAM A WINNER!

CHAPTER 1

LEARNING THE VALUE OF TEAMWORK

Teamwork is a plural process. It cannot be done by one person. When people come together to form groups, each member brings a personal set of knowledge, skills, values, and motivations. The whole is greater than the sum of its parts.
— ROBERT R. BLAKE
SPECTACULAR TEAMWORK
(JOHN WILEY & SONS)

Proving Teamwork Works

When the Eaton Corporation faced losing clients because of delivery problems, the manufacturer of electric components turned to a team approach to solve the problem. And rather than losing a client, said training coordinator and team facilitator Ronnie Moore, Eaton received a customer's "Certified Supplier" award.

When Loral Aeronutronic, which builds electro-optical devices for weapons systems, could not meet government quality standards, supervisors formed "Zone Defense Teams" to help workers understand how quality relates to their jobs. As a result, said Kenneth Tiernan, former vice president for product assurance, Loral went from losing up to 10 percent a year in sales to making a 10 percent profit.

The fact is that in most situations, two or four or six or more heads *are* better than one.

Jay Hall studied work teams for more than 20 years. In *Psychology Today,* he reported his research found that "when a group's final decision is compared to the independent points of view that the members held before entering the group, the group's effort is almost always better ... than even the best individual contribution."

One method Hall used to demonstrate the power of teamwork was a test developed by NASA that has frequently been used to demonstrate the advantages of group decision-making.

EXERCISE

LOST ON THE MOON

Have each member of your team take the test individually, then take the test as a group, discussing the points and submitting only a consensus answer. Compare individual scores and group scores with the answers provided by NASA.

Imagine your spaceship has just landed on the moon. You were scheduled to rendezvous with a mother ship 200 miles away, but the rough landing has ruined your ship and destroyed all the equipment on board, except for the 15 items listed subsequently.

The crew's survival depends on reaching the mother ship, so you must choose the most critical items available for the trip. Your job is to rank these 15 items in order of their importance for survival.

Make Your Team a Winner!

Place a 1 by the most important, and so on, with the least important ranked 15:

_____ box of matches

_____ food concentrate

_____ 50 feet of nylon rope

_____ parachute silk

_____ solar-powered portable heating unit

_____ two .45 caliber pistols

_____ one case of dehydrated milk

_____ two 100-pound tanks of oxygen

_____ map of the moon's constellation

_____ self-inflating life raft

_____ magnetic compass

_____ five gallons of water

_____ signal flares

_____ first-aid kit containing injection needles

_____ solar-powered FM receiver-transmitter

Make Your Team a Winner!

NASA's Answers

1. oxygen (most pressing survival need)
2. water (replacement for tremendous liquid loss on lighted side)
3. map (primary means of navigation)
4. food concentrate (for energy requirements)
5. FM receiver (for communication with mother ship)
6. nylon rope (for climbing cliffs)
7. first-aid kit (for medicines, vitamins, treatments; needles fit special aperture in NASA suits)
8. parachute silk (protection against sun's rays)
9. raft
10. flares (to signal mother ship when sighted)
11. pistols (possible means of self-propulsion)
12. dehydrated milk (bulkier duplication of food concentrate)
13. heating unit (not needed unless on dark side)
14. compass (worthless; magnetic field on moon is not polarized)
15. matches (no oxygen on moon; virtually useless)

How did your team score compared to your individual scores? Hall contends that, in most cases, the team's results will be closer to NASA's than any individual's. No matter what your results show, remember that the simple act of taking the test is a powerful tool for building your group's team spirit.

Getting Off to a Good Start

The first meeting of a team can be the most difficult because members need time to adjust to the situation and to feel comfortable. But the first meeting is also crucial. The future tone of the group is set in the first hour the team spends together.

The following are key activities that should be scheduled for that first meeting. Including them can help get your team off to a good, organized start:

1. Make introductions. Team members should introduce themselves, discuss their jobs, and describe any expertise they have. In addition, they might take a few minutes to discuss some personal information, such as outside interests or hobbies. Such a free exchange helps put everyone at ease and facilitates better work relationships. This is a good idea even when team members belong to the same unit.

2. Take minutes. It's important to have a record of business discussed at each team meeting. Take this opportunity to determine how the team will rotate the duty of taking minutes, and choose someone to handle the task for this first meeting.

3. Distribute supplies. Some organizations supply formal teams with supply kits containing pens or pencils, notebooks, transparencies, folders — sometimes even carrying cases. If no kit is provided, team members should be asked to bring necessary supplies to the next meeting.

4. Choose a team name. Choosing a name allows team members to relax and share ideas. Usually, it will break down some of the tension that exists between people meeting for the first time, and it will often bring out creative and humorous suggestions. Choosing a name identifies the team as a group and can be a first step toward building bonds among team members.

Make Your Team a Winner!

5. Choose a team leader. If a team leader hasn't already been appointed, the first meeting is the time for the group to select who will take this important role. The team leader will facilitate meetings, make assignments, and often resolve conflicts and act as a mediator between the team and project approvers or company management.

6. Review goals and objectives. Discussing the team's reason for existence is clearly the most important goal of the first meeting. Often a management representative will sit in for this segment to explain management's expectations and offer top-level support.

> **TIP**
>
> ## FRIENDLY EXCHANGES
>
> Sometimes it's difficult to quickly feel a sense of camaraderie with a group of relative strangers. To offset that initial awkwardness, consider following your first meeting with an informal, after-hours mixer. Getting together in a relaxed social setting can give you an opportunity to interact without the pressure of team expectations.

UNDERSTANDING YOUR MISSION

Once the new work team has been formed, its members need to understand exactly why the team has been established. That sounds simple enough. But business consultant James A. Shonk says teams get off to a bad start when they don't spell out the team's mission and the short-term goals needed to accomplish that mission.

How does a team's mission differ from its goals?

The team's mission is the overall reason the team exists. Goals are the short-term actions the team must carry out to fulfill its mission.

Shonk says even established teams should periodically review the team's overall purpose to ensure the team is on track.

MAKE YOUR TEAM A WINNER!

TAKE A MOMENT TO ...

WRITE A MISSION STATEMENT

The best way to ensure everyone on the team has a clear understanding of the mission is to work together to write a mission statement. Try to keep the statement brief and to the point. Once everyone agrees on the wording, copy the statement onto an overhead transparency or poster board so it can be displayed at every meeting. Then discuss the role each person will play in achieving the mission, so team members are aware of each other's functions within the team.

Making Resolutions

Resolutions aren't only for the new year. Whether your team is newly formed or a fixture your company can't do without, its members should resolve to

- **Support each other.** Of course, you can work as a team without feeling a sense of personal involvement. But why not get more out of the experience by letting yourself be genuinely concerned about your fellow workers?

- **Take chances.** Don't let your team grow complacent. Make the effort to find a new approach. Broadening your view and considering new ideas may help you reach the best solution.

- **Be patient with one another.** We all have bad days when we simply don't perform well. Be patient when a team member is just not "clicking." You'll appreciate having the breathing room yourself when you need it.

- **Accept your differences.** Your team may include people from various ethnic, socioeconomic, or political backgrounds. Perhaps one member climbed the ladder from the mail room, while another is a fresh-out-of-college MBA. Rather than letting your differences divide you, view them as an asset. Bringing together different voices gives your team a broader perspective. And utilizing your different experiences can help you find more creative solutions. If there are moments when your differences threaten to overwhelm you, sit back and take a deep breath. Then smile and appreciate that these differences make each member — and the whole team — unique.

Take a Moment to ...

Clarify Ground Rules

What's said here stays here. Be on time for team meetings. Resolutions require a majority vote. These are examples of team ground rules. Whether you're a professional athlete or a member of a work team, it's difficult to play the game if you don't know the rules. Discuss those things you feel are important to ensuring good working relationships and productivity. By asking each member to help write — and agree to — ground rules, you can quickly develop a sense of team trust and cooperation.

SETTING GOALS

Once your team has been formed, the top priority should be to set goals — the short-term actions the team must carry out to fulfill its overall purpose (such as saving money, cutting waste, developing a new product).

In his book *Teamwork: Involving People in Quality and Productivity Improvement* (Unipub), Charles Aubrey lists the following criteria for your goals:

- **Be specific.** A goal can be useful only if it specifies what is to be done and when.

- **Be measurable.** "Goals are intended to be a yardstick," Aubrey writes. Goals help evaluate the team's progress. That can only be done if goals allow progress to be measured in a specific way.

- **Be results-centered.** In determining goals, concentrate on the results, not on the activities to accomplish them.

- **Be realistic.** In its early stages, a team can make the mistake of being too optimistic about how soon results will be attainable. In the end, that will hurt a project because deadlines will be missed, work will fall behind, and enthusiasm will lag. "Realistic goals are goals that are within the bounds of the team setting them," Aubrey says.

- **Be challenging.** You'll want your goals to be realistic, but you should also make them slightly difficult to reach. "Setting aims high can motivate a team to achieve," Aubrey suggests.

Take a Moment to ...

Formulate a Plan

Follow these steps when setting goals for your project:

1. Review your team's mission statement to remind everyone of the team's reason for being.

2. Discuss the steps your team will have to take to achieve its mission.

3. Prioritize the steps to ensure you proceed in a logical order. For example, if your mission is to trim the department budget, you can't begin until you have a breakdown of the existing budget.

4. Once you've determined your first set of short-term goals, decide who will take responsibility for each. You may want to break your team into smaller work teams, each charged with achieving a single goal.

5. Agree upon deadlines for meeting each goal.

6. Set up a schedule for making interim reports. If a team member is having difficulty completing an assignment, these interim sessions can provide an opportunity to ask for help or guidance from the team as a whole.

7. As each goal is met, cross it from your list and repeat the process with a new set of goals. Don't make the mistake of resting on your initial success. Keep working toward short-term goals until the team achieves its overall mission.

STAYING ON TRACK

The team is in place and the goals are set. How can you be sure not to get off track? Consider these no-nonsense suggestions adapted from *Effective Project Planning and Management: Getting the Job Done* (Prentice Hall):

- **Establish checkpoints.** Checkpoints can help bring you back if your project begins to wander off in different directions.

- **Draw a picture of your project schedule.** A visual aid listing goals and their deadlines can help keep your project in focus.

- **Cheer each other.** One benefit of being on a team is having a ready-made support system. Help each other through the highs and lows. Teamwork is the glue that holds individual efforts together.

- **Keep everyone informed.** Post deadlines and meeting times. Discuss any unusual developments that may affect other team members.

- **Make the most of conflicts.** Rather than letting your conflicts divide you, use them as opportunities to find common ground to build on. Don't let personalities get in the way of issues.

- **Celebrate differences.** Each person has different talents and expertise. The beauty of working as a team is that you can draw on these individual differences to benefit the group.

- **Take risks and be creative.** When you reach a project roadblock, find a breakthrough by brainstorming ideas that are new and untried.

EXERCISE

TEST YOUR TEAM'S COMMITMENT

Your team is up and running. The following quiz can help you decide if your team is off to a good start. Answer **YES** or **NO**:

1. Do you believe work teams improve communication? _____
2. Do you believe working in teams increases productivity? _____
3. Has communication between you and your teammates improved? _____
4. Do you enjoy the work you do on the team? _____
5. Though you may not always agree with other team members, do you respect them overall? _____
6. Do you believe your team is making positive contributions to achieving the mission of your company? _____
7. Do you strive for good relations with your fellow team members? _____
8. Has your motivation increased? _____
9. Has working with others helped broaden your perspective? _____
10. Has teamwork helped bring out the best in you? _____

If you answered **YES** to at least eight questions, you have successfully accepted the teamwork approach. If you answered **YES** to five to seven questions, you are on your way. A low score indicates you are fighting the team concept.

What Would You Do?

You've just been asked to join a new work team on a key project. You're honored for the opportunity and feel up to the task. However, this will be your first experience outside the traditional hierarchical work structure and you're a bit nervous about how you should act at the first meeting. What can you as an individual do to help the team get off to a good start?

(Review "Getting Off to a Good Start" on page 6 for ideas.)

Team Activity

Do some of your teammates still feel uncomfortable collaborating with others? Try this team activity.:

Type the opening to a novel or fairy tale on a sheet of paper. Now give the paper to another team member with instructions to come to the next meeting with one *original* paragraph building on the first paragraph. Each team member will take turns writing additional paragraphs.

This activity will give the group an opportunity to have some fun and discover how creative their teammates can be. You probably won't write a masterpiece, but you can still have a lot of fun.

CHAPTER 2
BUILDING A STRONG TEAM

A long pull, and a strong pull, and a pull all together.
— CHARLES DICKENS

Generating Positive Team Spirit

Looking for a good team-building activity? How about competing together in a sled-dog race in Alaska?

Lloyd Gilbertson, owner of Caribou Creek Sled Dog School, uses sled-dog trips to teach teamwork and leadership skills to clients.

"Every situation we encounter has the opportunity for cooperation," Gilbertson says. "These trips encourage people to work together, to bring everyone's skills together in harmony."

Of course, not every team can take a trip to Alaska, but team building plays an important role in ensuring team success.

Here are some ways individual team players can help build team spirit:

- **Find a reason for working together.** Think of how the success of the team project will benefit you personally. What is it about your team goal that will bring you personal satisfaction? Help others discover the answers for themselves.

- **Care about and support other team members.** Fellow team members may withdraw and leave participation to others if they don't feel they are an integral part of the process. Encourage participation of others. Listen to their suggestions.

- **Have a sense of determination and commitment.** For a team effort to succeed, members need to feel the group goal is important. And they need to feel their success together is as valuable as any individual success they might achieve on other projects.

TAKE A MOMENT TO ...

DO SOME CHEERLEADING

One way to help build a strong team is to make people feel appreciated. Take time at the beginning of each meeting to acknowledge one another's accomplishments. You could also initiate a gold-star program in which a different member's contribution is recognized each week. It doesn't have to be a major accomplishment — it could be something as simple as thanking a teammate for bringing cookies to the team meeting.

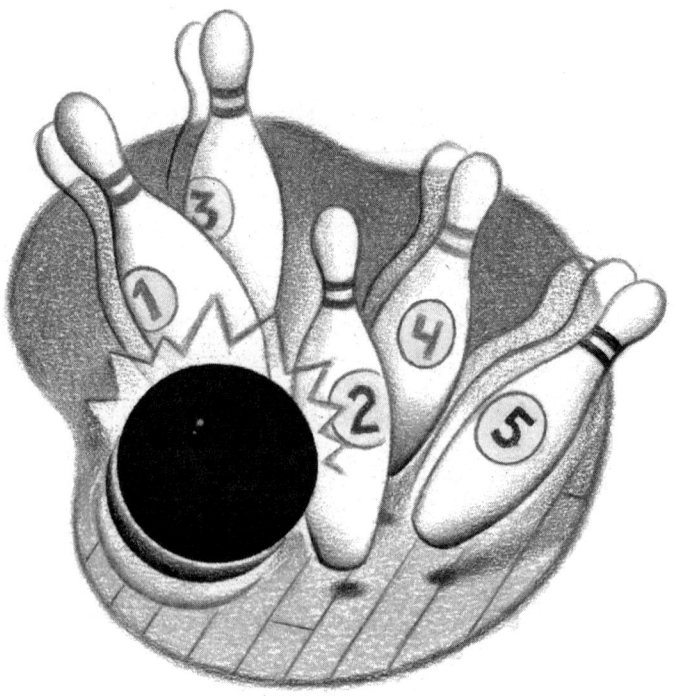

Tip

Field Trips

If your team is beginning to lose energy, consider planning a weekend getaway. You could take a fishing trip, go to a theme park, or even just get together for a backyard barbecue. Spending time together away from the pressures of your project can help you reconnect — and spark renewed creativity.

EXERCISE

ASSESS YOUR COHESIVENESS

The following questions can serve as a starting point in evaluating how well your team connects. For team members to maintain anonymity, the questions can be answered on paper and combined on a master sheet without attribution. Then the collective answers can be discussed and corrective action taken.

1. Do we trust each other? _____
2. Are we genuinely interested and concerned for each other? _____
3. Do we feel free to communicate openly? _____
4. Do we understand our team's goals? _____
5. Do we have a real commitment to these goals? _____
6. Do we make good use of all our abilities? _____
7. Do we handle conflict successfully? _____
8. Does everyone participate? _____
9. Do we respect our individual differences? _____
10. Do we enjoy being members of this team? _____

IMPROVING TEAM COMMUNICATION

Working as part of a team means learning to interact positively in a group setting. The following tips will help keep team communication lines open:

- **Try a roundtable approach.** To facilitate more open discussions, move chairs into a circle to help make each team member feel free to contribute.

- **Discuss roles and responsibilities.** Your team will become more cohesive as each member understands his or her relationship to the other members and the project as a whole. When team members discover the extent to which their work affects others, they are likely to become more quality-conscious.

- **Discuss problems and brainstorm solutions.** Team members should not have to struggle to solve problems individually. Working together to resolve difficulties can provide more creative solutions, help promote trust and cooperation — and give the team an opportunity to celebrate small victories.

Exercise

Start Talking

Does conversation lag in your team meetings? Does the team leader do most of the talking? Do team members answer inquiries in monosyllables? If so, team members could each bring one of the following to the next meeting:

- A short list of open-ended questions — those that *cannot* be answered simply with yes or no — pertaining to some aspect of the project or mission.
- A project-related anecdote.
- An article or report that touches on some aspect of the project.

To encourage group discussion, take turns sharing your contributions and soliciting comments and feedback from the rest of the group.

Maintaining Team Focus

Over time, even the best teams can begin to flounder — if they fail to monitor their progress. The following tips suggested by Ralph Barra's *Putting Quality Circles to Work* (McGraw-Hill) can help avoid some of the potential potholes on the road to completing your team's mission:

1. Look for consensus. Don't let team meetings become battlegrounds. Rather than focusing on winning the majority, try to achieve consensus. "Review the idea of consensus and emphasize a win-win situation versus a win-lose situation," Barra suggests.

2. Maintain enthusiasm for the team concept. To keep the focus on working together, discourage formation of interteam cliques. If some team members seem to be forming bonds that exclude others, assignments should be rotated to give everyone the opportunity to work together.

3. Stick with the plan. Don't lose sight of the goals you set at the beginning of your project. Though it's natural for a group to enjoy a degree of flexibility, Barra says, team members should be alert to wandering too far off track. Meeting regularly and setting meeting agendas is one easy way to maintain direction.

Finding Power as a Team

In its 1997 list of "America's Best Plants," *Industry Week* magazine noted that the 25 finalists all relied on self-directed or empowered teams to make their daily operations decisions. The following are three characteristics of these self-directed teams. Does your team demonstrate these key attributes?

1. Forward thinking. Finding solutions means understanding the need for change — and recognizing that old ways aren't coming back.

2. Risk-taking. Finding creative solutions often involves looking outside accepted boundaries and being willing to part from the norm.

3. Patience. Substantive change doesn't happen overnight. Team members must be willing to see the project through.

Determining Your Success

If you want to know whether your team is following the path to success, you need only look at your team characteristics. The following are characteristics of successful — and unsuccessful — teams:

- **Successful teams** ... have management support.
- **Unsuccessful teams** ... lack management support.
- **Successful teams** ... meet regularly and with purpose.
- **Unsuccessful teams** ... meet sporadically and have haphazard, or no agendas.
- **Successful teams** ... set goals and objectives.
- **Unsuccessful teams** ... struggle without direction.
- **Successful teams** ... clearly define the roles of each member and do not overlap responsibilities.
- **Unsuccessful teams** ... allow members to drift along with poorly defined duties and little responsibility.
- **Successful teams** ... choose strong leaders.
- **Unsuccessful teams** ... have poor leaders — or no leaders at all.
- **Successful teams** ... make decisions by consensus.
- **Unsuccessful teams** ... argue continually.
- **Successful teams** ... achieve solutions.
- **Unsuccessful teams** ... react to crises.

EXERCISE

EVALUATE YOUR TEAM

It's important that your team pause occasionally to evaluate itself as a group. Team members should take this quiz individually; then discuss the answers with each other. Answer **YES** or **NO**:

1. Has your most recent team project reduced costs, improved a product, helped improve time management, or resulted in some other type of measurable improvement? _____
2. Was the project completed on time? _____
3. Did your team leader accurately explain the project? _____
4. Were all members involved in the problem-solving process? _____
5. Was everyone kept abreast of the status of the project? _____
6. Did the team seek management approval as needed? _____
7. Did the team keep management informed? _____
8. Does your team value the concept of teamwork? _____
9. Has communication improved within the team as a result of the project? _____
10. Did communication improve between the team and management? _____

If your team members answered **NO** to more than five questions, you may want to spend more time on team-building techniques.

> ## What Would You Do?
>
> Your team leader does not offer encouragement to the group or help build team spirit in any way. As a result, the team suffers from indifference and a general lack of enthusiasm. What can you do to help strengthen the group?
>
> *(Review "Generating Positive Team Spirit" on page 18 for ideas.)*

Team Activity

Do you still feel you and your teammates have nothing in common? Try this team-building activity suggested by Memories Unlimited, a Florida firm that coordinates interactive events for companies:

Have each member of the team write down a personal tidbit no one else at the company knows, such as "I'm a Civil War reenactor" or "I play the violin." All the "secrets" are then gathered and read aloud so the team can try to guess which tidbit goes with which person. This can help teammates begin to look at each other in broader terms than just job title — and perhaps provide a basis for building camaraderie.

MAKE YOUR TEAM A WINNER!

CHAPTER 3

BECOMING A BETTER TEAM LEADER

A leader is a dealer in hope.

— **NAPOLEON**

LEARNING LEADERSHIP SKILLS

When Judy Dorr, a sales rep for Recycled Paper Greetings, needed to find an extra 48 feet of retail display space for her greeting cards, her sales manager worked with her to resolve the issue. Through a program that pairs managers with workers to tackle tough problems, Dorr's company ensures team leaders are involved participants in team projects.

This hands-on approach is one of the keys to successful leadership. But what are the other skills that make a good team leader?

In an interview in *Boardroom Reports,* team-building consultant Gisele Richardson said the skills that make an effective leader are not much different than those that make good team members. The most important, Richardson said, is the ability to bring out the best in others.

Consider the following leadership qualities and tips for developing them:

- **A sense of right and wrong.** Team leaders should initiate discussions on ethics and encourage the team to write a code of ethics. And they should affirm their commitment to the code by inviting teammates to speak up if leaders fall short of the standard.
- **Trustworthiness.** Team leaders should encourage trust among teammates by making clear that gossip among and about team members is not appropriate. When team members approach the leader with private issues, those issues should remain private.
- **Respect for other team members.** Team leaders must recognize that each team member has something valuable to contribute. They should be willing to share the load and allow others to take responsibility.
- **Eagerness to learn new skills.** Team leaders aren't know-it-alls. They must be willing to learn from other team members and ask questions that give members an opportunity to demonstrate their expertise.
- **Ability to give clear directions.** Team leaders should not be ambiguous when assigning duties. When making assignments, they should follow up with written confirmation or ask team members to verbally summarize the assignment as they understand it. This will help ensure there's no confusion about what's expected.
- **Willingness to praise good performance.** Team leaders should always take time to thank teammates for a job

well done. Giving credit where it's due encourages team members to continue giving their best.

- **Punctuality.** Team leaders should make a special effort to be on time for team functions. It's difficult to expect members to take meetings seriously if leaders don't.

- **A sense of humor.** It's one thing to take the project seriously — it's another to take yourself too seriously. Good team leaders are able to work on the project without draining the team's enthusiasm.

- **Ability to maintain focus.** Although a sense of humor can help lighten the load, it's not the function of a team leader to provide meeting entertainment. Leaders should approach meetings with a clear agenda — and stick to it.

- **Fairness.** In any team setting, there will always be some members who show more initiative and responsibility than others. Even so, the team leader cannot afford to play favorites. Strong team leaders should take the time to get to know each team member — and his or her strengths and weaknesses.

Take a Moment to ...
Make a Team Leader Wish List

What are you looking for in a team leader? In some cases, team leaders are chosen by management when the team is formed. In others, team members elect a leader, or the leadership duties are rotated. In these cases, teams have the opportunity to "shop" for the person with the strongest leadership qualities or to emphasize what qualities rotating leaders should demonstrate.

Before selecting a leader, your team should initiate a group discussion about positive leadership qualities. Using the attributes listed in the previous section as a guide, each team member can make a wish list of the five most important qualities he or she wants in a team leader. The lists can be combined and prioritized according to which qualities were named most.

Once the group has determined what qualities to look for, members will have an easier time choosing a person that meets the criteria. And if leadership duties are to be rotated, each person will know what's expected when his or her time rolls around.

Exercise

Test Your Leadership Potential

Do *you* have what it takes to be an effective team leader? Answer **YES** or **NO** to each of the following statements:

1. I am comfortable working in a team setting. _____
2. I feel I can handle more responsibility than I now have. _____
3. I get along well with my teammates. _____
4. I am confident speaking before a group. _____
5. I have a good understanding of the duties and responsibilities of each of my teammates. _____
6. I am well organized. _____
7. I have good relationships with project approvers and company managers. _____
8. I am self-motivated. _____
9. I am willing and able to work additional hours on my team's project. _____
10. I feel comfortable assigning duties to my teammates — and following up to see that they are carried out. _____

If you answered **YES** to at least seven statements, you are a good candidate to become a successful team leader. If you answered **YES** to five or fewer statements, you should spend more time working within a team structure and observing other leaders before taking on that role.

Meeting Tips for Team Leaders

One of the most obvious roles of a team leader is to facilitate meetings. Here are some simple tips to help meetings run more smoothly:

1. Start — and end — meetings on time.
2. Facilitate discussion — don't preside.
3. Share the agenda.
4. Post information for everyone to see on a flip chart or overhead transparency.
5. Be sure someone is keeping minutes.
6. Don't let the process become bogged down.
7. Set goals of what you'd like to see accomplished for each meeting.
8. At the conclusion, summarize the results of the meeting.
9. Repeat commitments, deadlines, and follow-up duties.
10. Encourage everyone to participate.

Sparking Team Creativity

In addition to facilitating team meetings, team leaders must also work to keep the group's enthusiasm from lagging — particularly on long-term projects. In his book *Managing Group Creativity* (American Management Association), Arthur G. VanGundy offers the following suggestions for building a creative work environment:

- **Encourage open expression of ideas.** Team leaders must reward efforts to be innovative and create a team atmosphere that gives new ideas a fair hearing. It's a leader's task to get everybody to open up.

- **Accept divergent ideas.** Team leaders must foster an environment where differences are celebrated. A work team that respects differences among its members is going to accomplish much more than any think-alike group.

- **Assist in developing ideas.** Team leaders must promote the benefits of brainstorming. When a team member comes up with a good idea but can't fully refine it, all team members should pitch in with questions and suggestions to help the idea's originator feel supported and to encourage further creative thinking.

- **Provide time for individual efforts.** As vital as teamwork is in any organization, people often need time alone to devise creative solutions. Team leaders should ask members to set aside time to reflect on key decisions before any group action is made final.

- **Furnish opportunities for personal growth.** In many cases, traditional approaches are not the best solutions. Team leaders should be willing to find ways to help members acquire new knowledge and skills, and they should encourage team members to consider innovative problem-solving techniques.

Tip

GET HELP TO MEET DEADLINES

Ensuring the team meets its deadlines and is served fully by each member are important facets of leadership. However, sometimes it's difficult to get teammates to cooperate without feeling like a nag. Here are two ways for team leaders to build the support of team members without antagonizing them:

1. Let the team decide deadlines. Team leaders who impose unrealistic deadlines are not taking into account the individual workloads and schedules of members. When your team begins its project, let everyone know the deadlines that are set in stone — then ask team members to set interim deadlines for meeting them.

2. Offer help. When you see a team member is running into trouble, ask what you can do to help. It may mean shifting some of the assignment to another member or making other adjustments to the schedule. At the very least, your concern will show that you are more interested in results than reprimands.

Avoiding Team Roadblocks

Regardless of the popularity and success of team initiatives, there will always be those who are more comfortable going it alone. And it's up to the team leader to find ways to bring those individuals into the fold. Here are a few common "anti-team" sentiments — and ways leaders can counter them:

- **I work better alone.** In an interview with *Psychology Today*, Roger and David Johnson, leading researchers on cooperative learning, said such thinking is common. They attributed this to school curriculums that emphasize individual achievement rather than working with others. "Teachers keep kids separate and quiet," explained Roger Johnson, "yet research on how kids best learn goes the opposite direction."

   In this case, success can be a good teacher. If those members who feel they work better alone get a chance to see how their productivity improves in a team setting, they may come around. The team leader could ask these members to work solo to solve a particular issue — then ask the team to refine the solution. Chances are, the team effort will be stronger than what was proposed by the lone member.

- **I have to stand out to succeed.** These individuals worry that their individual contributions will not be recognized in a team. Business psychologist Srully Blotnick found this to be the chief concern of 6,000 workers he interviewed about teamwork.

   For the team leader, the answer to this dilemma is simple. Take time at each meeting to recognize the *individual* efforts of team members. Make sure members are aware of each other's expertise to give everyone a chance to shine — and to encourage members to seek help from one another.

- **Teamwork is nice, but it doesn't really work.** Unfortunately, this sentiment is common among those who have been on unsuccessful teams, says Robert Blake in his book *Spectacular Teamwork* (John Wiley & Sons).

There isn't much team leaders can do to combat this thinking — except work hard to ensure the projects they direct are successful. For these naysayers, seeing is believing.

Exercise

Improve Your Leadership Effectiveness

The following quiz can help you determine whether you are utilizing the skills needed to be an effective leader in your team. Answer **YES** or **NO**:

1. Do you help the team establish goals? _____
2. Have you helped the team develop an agenda for each meeting? _____
3. Do you encourage participation from each member? _____
4. Do you create a positive atmosphere where members feel free to talk? _____
5. Do you help members communicate? _____
6. Do you keep conflict under control? _____
7. Do you play devil's advocate — bringing up opposing viewpoints so the team is exposed to all ideas? _____
8. Do you summarize key points after discussions? _____
9. Do you look for areas of consensus? _____
10. By the end of the meeting has the team reached a point of agreement on a course of action? _____

If you answered **YES** to eight or more questions, you are succeeding as an effective leader. If you scored lower, study the questions for tips on how to improve your leadership technique.

What Would You Do?

As team leader, you're finding it difficult to get an individual member to meet deadlines. As a result, the work group is falling behind schedule. Coming down hard on a member may produce short-term action but long-term animosity. What should you do instead?

(Review "Get Help to Meet Deadlines" on page 38 for ideas.)

Team Activity

If your team has trouble defining strong leadership qualities, try this activity:

Have each member of the team research a historical figure known for his or her leadership skills. The subjects may be military or political leaders, biblical figures, business tycoons — even film directors. Then ask each team member to give a short oral report describing his or her research topic's leadership qualities. Initiate a group discussion of the attributes shared by these successful leaders.

MAKE YOUR TEAM A WINNER!

CHAPTER 4

BEING A BETTER TEAM MEMBER

No person who is enthusiastic about his work has anything to fear from life.

— SAMUEL GOLDWYN

Performing Up to Par

Members of new product-development teams at Quantum Corporation are given one directive: Think like managers!

The reason, says Jane Creech, manager of management and organization development, is that Quantum's teams make million-dollar decisions every day. "We don't just give them a charter," Creech says of Quantum's team members. "We carefully select them, systematically develop them.... Such empowerment has been critical to team success."

However, not every organization makes Quantum's commitment to carefully nurture its work teams. In many cases, team members must look within to determine how to become better team players.

When was the last time you thought about the contribution *you* make to your team? Here's what some team members had to say when asked what special skills they offer their teams:

- *I always try to say something positive when someone else in the group makes a suggestion. There's something good about every idea, and I try to point that out first.*

- *In our company, it seems people get out of [attending] meetings a lot and it's pretty much OK if you do. But I don't think you should treat the team like that. I try to show up at all the meetings.*

- *I always pay attention and try to offer something. I like to give the group my best effort.*

Exercise

Are You a Responsible Team Member?

Are you an asset to your team — or a liability? The following quiz can help you gauge your effectiveness as a team member. Answer **YES** or **NO** to each question:

1. Do you attend almost every team meeting? _____
2. Do you arrive on time for team meetings and functions? _____
3. Do you come prepared? _____
4. Do you interact well with your teammates? _____
5. Do you contribute comments and suggestions during team discussions? _____
6. Are you willing to take on thankless tasks when necessary? _____
7. Do you stay focused on the team's goals and objectives? _____
8. Do you volunteer to help teammates with projects that are not your responsibility? _____
9. Do you take team activities seriously? _____
10. Do you fulfill obligations and meet deadlines? _____

If you answered **YES** to at least seven questions, your teammates probably enjoy working with you. If you answered **YES** to six or fewer questions, consider asking your team leader or a trusted teammate for an objective assessment of how you might improve your team performance.

Helping Teammates Improve Performance

With no formal training in how to be a good teammate, some team members lack the initiative to develop these skills on their own. In that case, it's up to the team to try to get the most from its members. Here are ways individuals or the team as a whole can help a teammate who doesn't toe the line:

- **Fellow members.** A problem teammate might react more positively when approached by a trusted friend. The friend should position the comments as concern rather than criticism — for example, by noting that the team member has been missing meetings or deadlines and asking if he or she needs help. This makes the team member aware that the lapses have been noticed — but avoids putting the individual on the defensive.

- **Team leader.** Often, the task of handling personnel — and personality — problems falls on the shoulders of the team leader. If so, the leader should approach the member in private and be matter-of-fact, explaining that when team members fail to meet their obligations, it affects the team as a whole. The team leader should avoid making accusations but should remind the individual what is expected — and be willing to listen to any explanations and offer help where needed.

- **The team.** Part of working in a team setting is being willing to work together as a unit to solve problems — even the problems of individuals. If one person is disrupting the function of the team as a whole, it may be necessary for the matter to be discussed openly with the entire group. Again, the team should avoid making accusations, be willing to listen, and offer help if needed.

Handling Diversity

Cultural, ethnic, and social diversity can breathe life into a team, inspiring creativity and uniqueness. Unfortunately, it can also cause conflict that undermines the team's mission. Learning how to work with people from different backgrounds is a challenge. But meeting that challenge will lead to greater productivity and the opportunity for personal growth.

To help team members learn to interact more positively with people of varying backgrounds, consultants Bob Abramms-Mezoff and Diane Johns, authors of *Success Strategies* (ODT Associates), offer the following simple tactics:

- **Put yourself in the other person's place.** Take a moment to consider what it must be like to move to a new country and learn a new language — or to live in a new region where the culture is different from your norm. Think about how uncomfortable you might be if you were the only person of your race or ethnic background in the room. Before you criticize someone for being "different," imagine if *you* were the different one.

- **Be frank in uncertain situations.** If you're in an unfamiliar situation or are met with an unusual custom and are unsure how to behave, ask. You are far less likely to offend by making an honest inquiry than by faking it and hoping for the best.

- **Follow the Golden Rule.** Regardless of the situation, if you treat others with the same courtesy you'd want to receive, you're likely to find positive results.

Take a Moment to ...
Find Common Ground

Regardless of the differences in their backgrounds, most human beings can find something in common — if they only try. To help teammates begin to find this common ground, try this activity:

At the next team meeting, initiate a discussion in which each person in turn shares an anecdote about an embarrassing moment. It's likely many people will have similar stories. Perhaps one handled the situation with humor; another with chagrin. But *all* will be able to imagine how it felt, for that moment, to be in the storyteller's shoes. This exercise can help lighten tension — and help people who thought they had nothing in common begin to see a common bond.

Tip

Good News

If you're looking for a way to boost team spirit *and* share important information, consider publishing a team newsletter that can be distributed within your team, to management, or even to other teams.

What would this newsletter include?

It could include articles about the team's progress in solving problems, news of team activities, and the impact the team's work has had on the organization. It also may include information about unique approaches or ideas generated by the team or gleaned from other sources — and perhaps even meeting minutes.

And the newsletter can feature "fun" items, such as a colorful logo, cartoons, a calendar of social events, birthdays of team members, interesting experiences, or motivational quotes.

Exercise

Do You Work Effectively on a Team?

Working as part of a team can be difficult for someone who has worked independently for a long time. Recognizing that you need to develop a team attitude is a good starting point, but the following quiz can help you refine your skills as a team member. Answer **YES** or **NO** to each question:

1. Do you give credit to others for their ideas? _____

2. Do you admit your mistakes? _____

3. Do you communicate your concerns, questions, and ideas to the team? _____

4. Are the opinions of your fellow team members important to you? _____

5. Do you make sure others in your group are not surprised by anything relating to the work you're doing? _____

6. Are you interested in the suggestions made by your fellow team members? _____

7. Are you friendly with the members of your team? _____

8. Do you support group decisions? _____

9. Do you encourage others to do their best? _____

10. Do you feel success belongs to everyone on the team? _____

If you answered **YES** to at least seven questions, you are a good team player. If you scored lower, study the questions for hints about how you can improve.

> ### WHAT WOULD YOU DO?
>
> Some members of your work team are not pulling their weight. Assignments are routinely late, forcing other team members to take up the slack. As a team member, how can you help resolve this situation?
>
> *(Review "Helping Teammates Improve Performance" on page 46 for ideas.)*

TEAM ACTIVITY

To get an idea of the qualities each member of your team values in teammates, try this activity:

Initiate a discussion session in which teammates toss out the attributes they appreciate in other team members — and those they don't. Have someone record the comments on a flip chart for everyone to review. Once team members have determined the qualities they will — and won't — accept in their teammates, the list can be used to help refine team ground rules as discussed in Chapter 1.

MAKE YOUR TEAM A WINNER!

CHAPTER 5

UNDERSTANDING TEAM DYNAMICS

When you take the time to understand the needs and expectations of others, they pay you back many times over.
— CRAIG HICKMAN

SEEING THE PIECES OF THE PUZZLE

Understanding team dynamics is nothing more than understanding the individual personalities that make up the team and how those personalities interact.

Since the 1940s when social scientists first began studying work teams, they have observed the various roles individual members play in their group. Though the experts don't necessarily agree on exactly how many roles there are and how to name them, 10 general personality types have been identified:

1. Task Leaders. These individuals may not be designated team leaders, but they still play a natural leadership role. They are nuts-and-bolts, roll-up-the-sleeves types.

2. Emotional Leaders. These are the team counselors, the emotional heartbeat of any group. They are good listeners, the people team members go to for help with personal problems.

3. **Tension Releasers.** Meet the group entertainers. These are the people teams can count on to break the tension with a well-placed one-liner.

4. **Information Providers.** Of course, no team is complete without the researchers — the folks who have all the details at their fingertips. The problem for these individuals, however, is that the group may take advantage of their skills by giving them most of the grunt work.

5. **Devil's Advocates.** There's one in every crowd — the Devil's Advocate who always says, "But what if ...." These people offer their teams a voice of caution, but usually in a non-threatening way.

6. **Questioners.** If Devil's Advocates always say, "But what if ... ," Questioners are always ready with the five W's: who, what, when, where, and why. These are the team members who constantly seek clarification and more information.

7. **Observers.** Observers tend to quietly take it all in, speaking only when they have something relevant to say. And when they do contribute, people listen.

8. **Listeners.** To Listeners, paying attention is not a passive activity. They listen attentively, regularly sum up others' viewpoints, and keep discussions on track.

9. **Recorders.** Recorders have little interest in being active group participants, preferring instead to just take notes or keep team minutes.

10. **Self-Servers.** Self-Servers are the team bad apples. They constantly question opinions in a nonsupportive way, and unlike Devil's Advocates, are disruptive rather than cautious. They are only concerned with their personal interests.

TAKE A MOMENT TO ...
LOOK AT ROLES WITHIN YOUR TEAM

Are you a Tension Releaser? Is your teammate a Devil's Advocate? To see how various personality types contribute to the dynamics of your team, try the following exercise:

Make a list of the 10 personality types to distribute to each member of the team. Then ask each member to write beside the personality types the names of those team members, including themselves, who fit each type. (It is possible to have more than one of each type on a team or to have a single person fit more than one trait.)

Afterward, compare your lists and use it as a basis for discussion. Do most team members see themselves as others see them? How might each team member use this feedback to build on strengths — or improve weaknesses? Are there key roles — such as the cautionary Devil's Advocate — that no one fills?

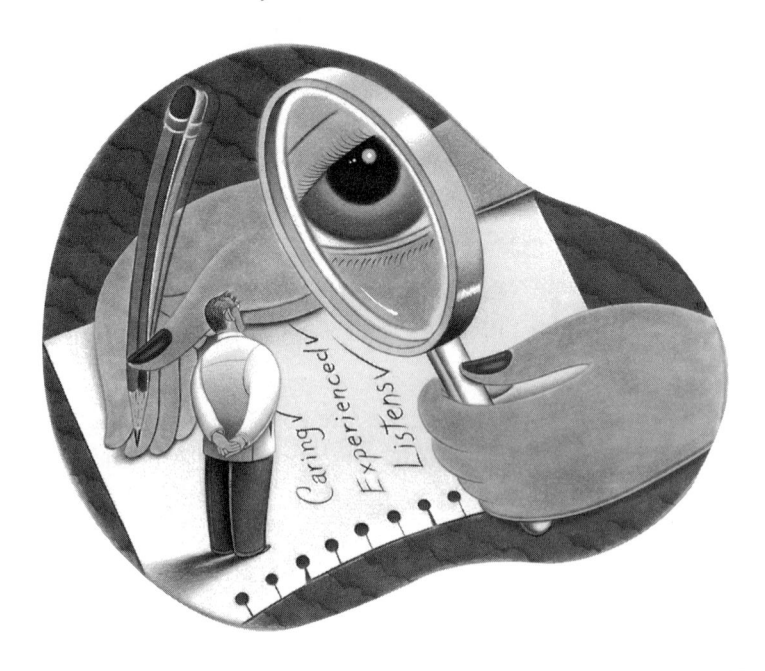

DETERMINING YOUR TEAM'S PERSONALITY

Just as individual personalities make up a work team, the work team — as a group — develops a personality of its own. Learning to recognize the characteristics that make up this collective personality can help your team more readily identify its strengths and weaknesses. The result: the ability to make better use of your team's assets — and more easily overcome its liabilities.

To give you a starting point for assessing your team's personality, consider the following personality types suggested by the work of management consultant Charles Aubrey:

- **Partyers.** Welcome to *Animal House*. This group has great energy — but it's often misdirected, Aubrey says. Partyers tend to focus more on social activities than project goals. There is no obvious task orientation. Aubrey suggests this team find a strong leader to help keep members on course.

- **Grindstones.** Grindstones are the polar opposite to Partiers in that they are extremely task oriented. Unfortunately, however, Grindstones are so set on steering a straight course that they lack imagination and tend to get bogged down in minutiae, checking and double-checking every detail. The solution? Grindstones should devote some time to team-building exercises that emphasize creativity and nontraditional problem-solving.

- **Stars.** Aubrey describes Stars as high achievers with a great deal of enthusiasm. However, their desire to shine for management makes them less likely to risk skewering company sacred cows to achieve a better project outcome. The real danger is that management could hold Stars up as the ideal group and neglect less visible or more avant garde efforts. Stars can overcome this by being willing to engage in some risk-taking to find more creative solutions.

- **Firecrackers.** Like Stars, Firecrackers have high energy and enthusiasm — but they are also willing to question authority. "Firecrackers want to get something done quickly to change or improve the organization," Aubrey says. On the negative side, Firecrackers tend to be somewhat erratic, wasting energy on short-lived stops and starts. They can improve their performance by setting deadlines that ensure steady progression toward meeting team goals.

Take a Moment to ...
Assess Your Team's Personality

Just as you discussed the roles each individual plays within your team, it can be beneficial to take a hard look at your team's personality as a group.

Using the categories listed in the previous section as a guide, initiate a group discussion to determine your team's personality. Are you a team that would rather organize a softball game than a goal-setting session? Are you management's darlings — never questioning the traditional way of doing things? Does your enthusiasm quickly wane in the face of deadlines and commitments? If so, perhaps your team needs to reevaluate its priorities, select a new team leader, or make other role adjustments.

By making an objective assessment of your team's personality, you can provide yourselves an opportunity to make improvements.

Understanding Group Communication

For your team to work together successfully, it pays for the members to know a little about communication. An understanding of the basic styles people use to communicate can help teammates better understand each other — and interact more effectively.

Stuart M. Schmidt, a professor of human resources, and David Kipnis, a professor of psychology, have studied the different communication styles that exist within small work groups. In one study, reported in *Psychology Today*, they broke down six strategies used by members of small work groups when they want to get their way:

1. Reason. With this strategy, members back up their assertions with detailed plans.

2. Assertiveness. Assertive individuals rely on repetition to get their points across.

3. Friendliness. Friendly teammates get their way by making others feel important.

4. Coalition. Some members strengthen their position by developing alliances with other team members.

5. Authority. Rather than approach the team, some members target the team leader, or even outside management.

6. Bargaining. Teammates who bargain are willing to trade something they have — for example, volunteering to help another teammate complete a project on schedule — to get what they want.

Teammates may employ each of these strategies at different times. But, according to Schmidt and Kipnis, people often fall into specific style categories when it comes to their communication within the team. The following list expands on styles suggested by the professors:

- **Shotgunners.** Shotgunners refuse to take no for an answer. Instead, they try to bully others into seeing their side.

- **Tacticians.** Tacticians use reason and logic to bring others around.

- **Ingratiators.** Ingratiators play politics and rely on flattery to win allies.

- **Straddlers.** Rather than actively try to convert people to one view or another, Straddlers stay firmly planted in the middle. They don't cause problems — but they also don't contribute.

- **Trailblazers.** Trailblazers have the courage of their convictions, but they don't try to manipulate or bully others into their way of thinking. They influence others by demonstrating confidence in their positions — and themselves.

Exercise

What's Your Style?

Are you a Shotgunner, a Trailblazer, or a Straddler? To find out, read the following scenarios and responses. Place a **5** beside the response you would most likely give, a **4** beside your next choice, and so on, with a **1** beside your least likely response.

1. Your team is trying to decide on a controversial proposal for solving the company's budget woes. You ...

    a. prefer to sit back and listen to the discussion rather than taking issue. _____

    b. feel it's important to bring others around to your side. _____

    c. prepare a report outlining the advantages of your position. _____

    d. calmly state your case and wait to see where the dust settles. _____

    e. compliment your teammates on their reasoning skills before explaining your position. _____

2. Your team has been struggling to meet deadlines, and several members have been arriving late for team meetings. You ...

    a. mind your own business. _____

    b. take the initiative to tell the team you don't appreciate such sloppy behavior. _____

    c. keep an attendance log and a record of missed deadlines to present during a team discussion. _____

d. suggest the team work together to set ground
   rules for how the team will operate. _____

e. quietly enlist the support of other teammates
   before confronting the worst offenders. _____

3. Management is elated over the success of your project, and it's possible some team members will be in line for promotion. You …

   a. would love to reap the benefits of the team's
      success but don't want to be accused of taking
      too much credit. _____

   b. remind everyone about the important role you
      played in the success of the project. _____

   c. keep a record of each team member's contribution
      to ensure everyone gets appropriate credit. _____

   d. feel secure in the role you played and are
      content to share glory with the team. _____

   e. treat your team leader and key managers to
      lunch. _____

4. Your team has decided to develop a code of ethics. You …

   a. feel it's important to have a code of ethics but
      don't want to be accused of telling others how
      to behave. _____

   b. have a clear idea what should be included in
      the code and intend to see that your suggestions
      are heeded. _____

   c. go to the library to research how other companies handle ethical resolutions. _____

d. have a strong personal code of ethics and are happy to help write a team code. _____

e. see this as an opportunity to become team watchdog as a way to make points with the team leader. _____

Now, total your responses for a, b, and so on and record your totals here:

Straddler	a	_____
Shotgunner	b	_____
Tactician	c	_____
Trailblazer	d	_____
Ingratiator	e	_____

If you scored highest as a Straddler, you might want to make a greater effort to assert yourself. On the other hand, if you're a Shotgunner, you need to spend more time listening to others. Being a Tactician can be positive — if you don't let over-reliance on data keep you from being open to creative choices. If you are an Ingratiator, you may want to put more effort into being an effective teammate — and less into making points with others. And if you are a Trailblazer — congratulations and keep up the good work!

Tip

THE RIGHT SIGNALS

If you don't feel teammates take you seriously, perhaps you're sending out the wrong nonverbal messages, messages that convey a negative attitude toward your team. Take a moment to evaluate how you interact with your teammates. Do you …

- Always arrive late or leave early? Few people are always on time. But if keeping irregular hours is a habit, you're telling people you don't care enough about the team to give it the time it deserves.
- Ignore the dress code? Individuality is an admirable quality. But if your appearance is sloppy or inappropriate, it can signal disrespect for the team.
- Avoid helping others? Being a good team player means being willing to lend a helping hand. If you aren't, you're telling others "team" is not a priority.
- Take frequent breaks, turn in sloppy work, or miss deadlines? Not taking your work seriously is the same as not taking the team seriously.

Speaking the Team Language

Small groups that work together daily, or even less frequently, usually develop their own abbreviated language to discuss their activities and facilitate decision-making.

"Over time, groups develop an elaborate array of idioms that are based upon the history of the group," explain John F. Cragan and David W. Wright in their book *Communication in Small Group Discussions* (West Publishing Co.).

The authors note that this group language is an indication of the relationships team members develop. It reflects the way team members include each other and also the degree of goodwill that exists among members who share in the language.

However, they say, problems can develop when team members mistakenly think everyone speaks their language and release public communiques that contain team ideas encased in team jargon.

Another complication arises when new members join the team. Cragan and Wright discuss an example in which one team advised bewildered new members "not to be a Greenwood" — a reference to a former team member who regularly came late to meetings.

"It may take a new member several weeks or months to uncover the important incidents in a group's past that give meaning to verbal expressions that punctuate the group's daily discussions," the authors write.

They suggest team leaders and members should explain jargon to new members. Learning to understand the new language will help the new member feel included in the team.

WELCOMING NEW MEMBERS

New members joining an existing team face more difficult obstacles than just learning team jargon. The team already works comfortably together, and members have a bond that may seem difficult for even an outgoing newcomer to penetrate.

Take the case of Sara Hypothetical. Sara is not outgoing — in fact, she's obviously shy. It would be easy for the team to just ignore Sara and continue working as before. But Sara's team leader is conscious of the potential benefits of bringing new ideas into the old mix.

During group discussions, the leader makes time to observe Sara. And, when it appears she has something to say, the leader asks her opinion. To the group's surprise, Sara contributes several useful suggestions. Other team members follow suit in asking Sara's input. Soon, she begins asserting herself without coaxing. And by working to involve her in team discussions, Sara's team leader and teammates have gained a valuable team asset.

Tip

Roll Out the Welcome Mat

Consider the following tips for making new members feel welcome on your team:

- **Start slowly.** Take time to get to know new members and integrate them into group activities. Don't expect newcomers to contribute top-notch suggestions the first day.

- **Offer frequent reassurance.** Newcomers are bound to feel somewhat out of place at first. Help them feel more comfortable by offering positive feedback when they contribute or acknowledging any expertise they bring to the project.

- **Involve newcomers in discussions.** Once newcomers have become familiar with the project, ask their opinions in order to draw them into team discussions.

EXERCISE

DO YOU FOLLOW THE CODE?

In most teams, there is an informal code by which members conduct themselves to ensure mutual cooperation and respect. Take the following quiz, answering **YES** or **NO**, to determine how your team fares:

1. Do most team members arrive on time for meetings? _____
2. Do most members come prepared? _____
3. Do members listen to one another in team discussions? _____
4. Do most members fully participate? _____
5. Are all members treated equally? _____
6. Do most members work to achieve consensus and respect team decisions? _____
7. Do most members try to hear out one another if there is a disagreement? _____
8. Are most members willing to pitch in with arranging chairs or clean-up duties? _____
9. Do most members adhere to the team's ground rules or code of ethics? _____
10. Do most members regularly attend meetings? _____

If you answered **YES** to at least eight questions, your teammates probably share mutual respect and interact well together. If your team scored lower, consider engaging in team-building exercises or setting ground rules for team conduct.

> ## What Would You Do?
>
> Your team has just been formed but hasn't had time to develop into a cohesive unit, and it's difficult to assess who will end up taking various key roles. Nevertheless, your first project must be completed in less than a month. What can your teammates do to more quickly get a sense of team dynamics?
>
> *(Review "Seeing the Pieces of the Puzzle" on page 54 for ideas.)*

Team Activity

It's often said that, after a while, spouses begin to look alike. Team members, on the other hand, begin to sound alike. As previously discussed, many teams develop a language that outsiders have difficulty understanding. Does your team have its own secret code? Try this activity to find out:

At each team meeting, assign one member to jot down any unusual words or phrases that apply only to your team or project. After several meetings, compile the notes and read them aloud to the group. You'll probably be surprised to discover you and your teammates have a language all your own.

CHAPTER 6

IMPROVING TEAM MEETINGS

*It's easy to get good players. Gettin' 'em to play together —
that's the hard part.*

— **CASEY STENGEL**

Building a Better Meeting

The last good meeting I attended was when our ad team was about a month old. We had gotten over the initial "shy" period, where no one said much, and now we were really flying. Everyone was enthusiastic and the level of energy was fantastic. I wish we could have kept everything at that level, but now everyone seems to be settled into routine.

— ED, ADVERTISING ACCOUNT EXECUTIVE

The last good meeting I attended was, unfortunately, not a meeting I was participating in. Our class was sitting in on a meeting of a team of neurologists at our hospital. They were discussing a patient that one of the doctors had trouble diagnosing. It was fascinating to watch them go back and forth with ideas. There seemed to be no egos involved — they were really looking for a solution and not trying to outdo each other. I came away really respecting them and their work.

— JEFF, MEDICAL STUDENT

The last good meeting I attended? I can't think of a meeting that was very good!

— DIANE, PERSONNEL ADMINISTRATOR

Regardless of the type of project your team is tackling, there's one thing you can't escape — the team meeting. Somewhere out there, there may be teams whose meetings are crackling with excitement and running over with productive discussions. But most just seem to plod along.

The truth is, for many teams, meetings are boring, boring, boring. And worse, they're unproductive. The good news is that with a little effort, team members can breathe life into dead meetings. Consider the following tips suggested by Bob Nelson, co-author of *We've Got to Start Meeting Like This: A Guide to Successful Meeting Management* (JIST Works):

- **Prepare to contribute.** Team members should jot down discussion ideas before each meeting — whether or not they expect to be asked for input. Members should review the agenda in advance and check for areas in which they can contribute.

- **Don't overwhelm the group with information.** "Make one point at a time," Nelson says. Members who make what Nelson calls "double- or triple-headed comments" will only succeed in sending discussions off on tangents.

- **Be assertive and confident.** When members have something to say, they should speak up and get to the point. Mumbling and rambling puts others to sleep.

- **Back opinions with facts.** The quickest way to lose control of a meeting is to let it deteriorate into a pointless bull session. Members should make a conscious effort to offer substantive, fact-based information rather than just off-the-cuff opinions.

- **Listen actively to the discussion.** "Listeners who stay in touch with the whole discussion tend to have a more complete and accurate grasp of what happened at the meeting," Nelson says. As a result, their contributions tend to be more relevant than those of members who just want to make points.

- **Send positive nonverbal signals.** Team members should try to avoid sending unconscious signals — such as frowning or fidgeting — that could make other teammates feel they disagree with, or are bored by, the group's discussion.

TAKE A MOMENT TO ...

FIND WAYS TO COMBAT MEETING APATHY

What would it take to make your meetings sizzle? The best way to find out is to ask the team.

Ask everyone on the team to come up with an idea to spice up meetings — an idea that won't take away from the business being conducted. Encourage imaginative solutions. For example, how about creating an award for the best speaker or for the most creative idea? Or how about initiating "beat the clock" brainstorming sessions in which participants try to throw out as many ideas as they can in two minutes?

Team members can then discuss the suggestions and select those they'd like to try.

Finding a Facilitator

Of course, the primary responsibility for the tone of a meeting falls on the facilitator. The facilitator may be the team leader, or the role may rotate.

Once the team selects a facilitator, it is up to that individual to complete the following tasks:

- Schedule a time and place for the meeting.
- Prepare and distribute a meeting agenda.
- Coordinate any necessary meeting aids.
- Prepare a list of discussion topics.
- Arrange for speakers or presenters.

Facilitators are the people who must see that meetings begin and end in a timely fashion. They must make sure someone is taking minutes and, before adjourning, make plans for the next meeting. But most important, they must steer the course of the discussion, ensuring that everyone participates and all proposed topics are covered.

In short, facilitators are the meeting emcees — the people who keep everything running smoothly *and* keep the audience interested. In that sense, the same qualities that make a scintillating public speaker can also serve a meeting facilitator.

Sue Gaulke, presentation-skills coach and author of *101 Ways to Captivate a Business Audience* (AMACOM), says the most important quality a presenter can have is enthusiasm.

Facilitators also need to be prepared and knowledgeable about their subjects, Gaulke says. "People want information to be presented in a logical, well-organized way."

And what least impresses an audience? According to Gaulke, it's "trying to cram dry information down their throats" or speaking in a monotone.

Tip

Meeting Agenda

One way for a meeting facilitator to ensure everyone is present and prepared for a meeting is to send out a pre-meeting agenda. The agenda should include the following:

- Date, starting time, and place of the meeting.
- Subject of the meeting and items to be addressed.
- List of items members should bring to the meeting.
- List of proposed speakers and time allotted for each.

TAKE A MOMENT TO ...

JUDGE YOUR MEETINGS

Here's a simple test to help facilitators determine whether or not they keep their meetings on course:

Try writing a short memo briefly summarizing what is to take place in a particular meeting *before* you hold the meeting. In other words, write the meeting minutes before the meeting takes place. First, set your meeting objectives. Then define what needs to take place to meet your definition of success. After the meeting, compare your minutes to what actually happened.

BRINGING MEETINGS UNDER CONTROL

What if your meetings seem to be spiraling out of control, and you aren't the facilitator? You can still help your team achieve its meeting goals.

Suggest to the group that specific amounts of time be allotted to each agenda item. For example, discussions of new assignments may be scheduled for 10 minutes. Then, when you see a session is running late, you can help get it on course by referring to the time schedule.

TIP

CHAT TIME

If your team wastes too much meeting time on socializing, try organizing a weekly team outing — such as a midweek lunch or a Friday evening happy hour. This activity can give team members time to interact socially — without infringing on important meeting time.

The Meeting Overrunneth

If allowing meetings to run overtime is a problem for your team, consider the following suggestions:

- **Start on time.** A chief reason meetings run long is that there is a lax attitude about starting on time, says Jim Davidson, author of *Effective Time Management* (Human Sciences Press). Members drifting in late must be brought up to speed, causing the group to lose focus — and the meeting to run long. Set a start time for meetings and stick to it. Don't cover old ground to accommodate tardy members.

- **Stick to the agenda.** Allot time for each item on the agenda, and don't let discussions run over. "It's a fallacy to think decisions are better ones because everyone has participated with lengthy discourses," Davidson writes. "Lengthy discussion can cloud the central issue." If one item requires more discussion time, make room for it on the next meeting agenda.

- **Form ad hoc committees.** If one item does warrant special attention, consider forming an ad hoc committee to study the matter and report back to the team as a whole. This can save hours of meeting time, Davidson says.

- **Look forward to the next meeting.** Keep a record of who is doing what for the next meeting and make sure all members know their assignments. This head start can help keep the next meeting on schedule, too.

TIP

DOG DAYS

The success of your team meetings could depend on the day the meetings are held.

Accountemps, a temporary agency, asked personnel directors of the nation's 1,000 largest corporations what day of the week is most productive for employees. The result? Tuesday received 53 percent of the vote, followed by Wednesday with 19 percent.

Surveyors also asked which day employees were least productive. Friday topped the list with 59 percent of the vote, followed by Monday with 33 percent.

Scheduling meetings around these high and low points could increase effectiveness.

Exercise

Beat Meeting Deadlock

One surefire way to get a meeting to run long is for your team to reach a decision-making impasse. To break the silence, consultant James H. Shonk recommends a technique called "snapshot."

In *Effective Meetings Through Teamwork* (Shonk & Associates), he suggests going around the room and asking each person to take no more than 30 seconds to respond to such questions as: *What do you think the problem is? What should be our next step? What did you get out of the last discussion?* Getting team members to react quickly can bring new ideas out in the open that otherwise would never have been considered. And that can break deadlocks quickly.

Using Audiovisual Aids

You have an important idea you want to convey at the next meeting of your work team. What's the best format? Presentation-skills coach Sue Gaulke recommends using visual aids to liven up meetings. Here are some choices:

- **Flip charts.** One of the most common ways to present information to smaller groups is to write it on large flip charts. A presenter can prepare the charts ahead of time, or a team member can record key discussion points during the meeting. Be sure to use a dark marker for better visibility — and write legibly.

- **Overhead transparencies.** Transparencies are a useful and cost-effective way to present meeting information. To ensure readability, use large type, avoid elaborate typefaces and styles, and don't cram too much information on one transparency. If you'll be speaking to a large group, try out the transparency before the meeting to make sure it can be easily read from the back of the room.

- **Slides.** If you're making a formal presentation — perhaps to project approvers — and have some room in your team budget, consider preparing slides. Many marketing or communications departments have the resources to put together an in-house slide presentation, or you can hire an outside designer. As with transparencies, avoid decorative type that may be difficult to read, and don't put too much information on one slide.

Take a Moment to ...
Create a Colorful Slide Presentation

There's not much point in spending money on a slide presentation that just mirrors everything the speaker says. Instead, consider creating slides that are entertaining — and memorable.

Before your next presentation, brainstorm ideas for slides that complement, rather than repeat, the information being presented. For example, how about cartoons that make your point in a humorous way? Just be aware that the more creative a slide, the more expensive it will be. Be sure your team budget can cover the costs.

EXERCISE

GET MORE OUT OF TEAM MEETINGS

Attitudes can make or break a meeting. If you attend a meeting with the attitude that it is a waste of time — it will be.

The following quiz can help you see how to get more out of meetings. Answer **YES** or **NO** to each question:

1. Do you always read the meeting agenda in advance? _____
2. Do you prepare in advance? _____
3. Do you get enough sleep the night before a meeting? _____
4. Do you avoid a heavy lunch so you don't experience a slump in afternoon meetings? _____
5. Do you contribute to each meeting? _____
6. Do you try to help meetings stay on track? _____
7. If you miss a meeting, do you get a fellow team member to bring you up to date? _____
8. Do you take notes at meetings? _____
9. Do you volunteer to make meeting presentations? _____
10. Do you speak positively about your team's meetings to others? _____

If you answered **YES** to at least eight questions, you're getting the most out of your team meetings. Six or seven is average. A lower score means you need to remember that meetings are what you make them.

What Would You Do?

It's your turn to act as facilitator for your team's next meeting. Lately the meetings have been dry. The discussion lags, and the group seems to have difficulty following the agenda. How can you make the meeting you facilitate more lively — and productive?

(Review "Building a Better Meeting" on page 72 for ideas.)

Team Activity

Do your teammates still think it's easy to facilitate a meeting? Try this activity to demonstrate that taking center stage isn't always what it's cracked up to be:

Ask teammates to videotape or make notes while watching stand-up comics perform on late-night television. Now, have each teammate take turns "performing" the routine for the group. (Be sure to avoid vulgar or profanity-laden routines that might offend team members.) Even with "professional" material, it's not always easy to please a crowd.

MAKE YOUR TEAM A WINNER!

CHAPTER 7

COPING WITH CONFLICT

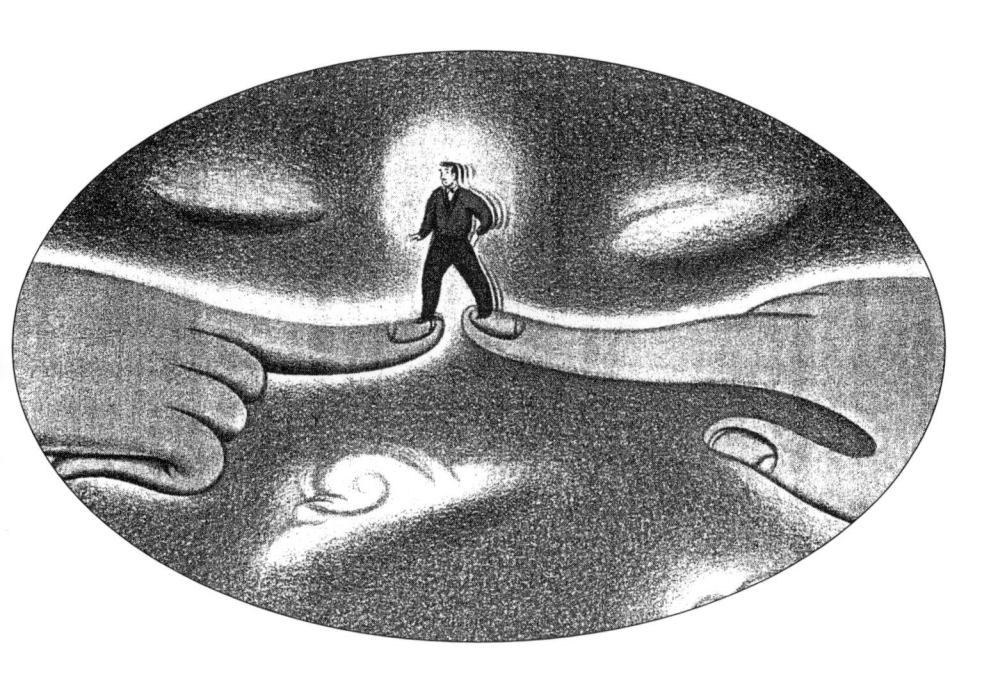

*Some folks are so contrary that if they fell in a river,
they'd insist on floating upstream.*

— JOSH BILLINGS

Understanding Conflict

Regardless of how well your team interacts, there are going to be moments of conflict. Conflict can be the result of personality differences, cultural diversity, incompatible project goals — even hidden agendas. Whatever the cause, trying to avoid conflict altogether is pointless. The better choice is to develop skills for resolving conflicts.

The following strategies for handling conflict are adapted from *The Team Leader's Idea-A-Day Guide* (Dartnell) by Susan Fowler Woodring and Drea Zigarmi:

1. Accepting. Sometimes it's important to accept things you don't like in order to achieve a common goal. The important thing is to choose your battles carefully. If the stakes are low, being able to put your concerns aside for the greater good can serve you well — and help you build allies — in the long run.

2. Creating. Before a disagreement becomes serious, it's a good idea to have all parties step back, look at what each is trying to accomplish, and prioritize these goals. Then the team can work together to create a new solution that draws the best from each proposal.

3. Retreating. When a discussion becomes so heated it threatens to cause long-term damage to the team, sometimes it's best to do nothing — at least for the moment. Initiate a cooling-off period to give all parties time to calmly consider the problem, and come together again only when you all feel you're ready to progress.

4. Contesting. When the stakes are high and you strongly believe in your position, that is the time to stand your ground. Of course, to achieve success, you have to hope other members are more willing to compromise than you are.

5. Modifying. When all else fails and you are left with a stalemate, it may be time for someone — perhaps an outside mediator — to decide on a compromise. In this case, everyone will get something — but no one will get everything.

TAKE A MOMENT TO ...

DECIDE HOW IMPORTANT IT IS TO WIN

When you are caught up in a conflict that threatens to divide the group and undermine your project, before you proceed, take time to review the issue.

On a sheet of paper, write out your position and list its advantages. Next, write its disadvantages — and be as objective as possible.

Now, write out your adversary's position and list *its* advantages and disadvantages — again, being as honest as possible.

Finally, review the information and list how your adversary's proposal might overcome the disadvantages in your proposal.

When you publicly argue a point, sometimes pride takes over. By doing this exercise away from the pressure of an audience, you may be able to see the merit in your adversary's position. And perhaps you'll find a way to combine your opposing ideas to find a more creative solution than either of you imagined.

WATCHING OUT FOR HIDDEN AGENDAS

Sometimes an undercurrent of tension in a work group has no obvious source. If so, hidden agendas may be at work. Hidden agendas can stem from prejudice, personality conflicts, or leadership aspirations. They are not always easy to spot, but there are several steps teams can take to work them out:

- **Watch for hidden agendas.** Don't try to pretend hidden agendas don't exist. They may lie under the surface, but everyone at one time or another reacts to a situation for selfish reasons.

- **Openly acknowledge hidden agendas.** One way to bring hidden agendas to the surface is to say something like, "I wonder if we've all been honest about our feelings on this matter? Would anyone like to add anything?" A little more discussion time may expose these underlying issues.

- **Don't embarrass anyone.** Don't chide others about their hidden agendas. Team communication can come to a halt if people are singled out in this manner.

- **Don't judge.** Is the atmosphere on your team one in which members feel they can say what's on their minds without being judged? If so, hidden agendas are more likely to come to the surface and be worked out for the benefit of the team.

DEALING WITH DIFFICULT PEOPLE

Not all conflicts are rooted in opposing positions, or even hidden agendas. Sometimes the problem is just dealing with difficult people.

When it comes to difficult people, the best offense may be a strong defense, says author Robert M. Bramson in his book *Coping with Difficult People* (Dell). Here are Bramson's suggestions for handling what he considers three of the most difficult types of people to work with:

- **Sherman Tanks.** Sherman Tanks are always on the attack. These are the scream-and-holler types who don't attack behavior — they attack people. "Sherman Tanks have strong needs to prove to themselves and others that their view of the world is right," Bramson says. He recommends standing up to them — without fighting. Give them a moment to blow off steam; then cut in. State your opinions and perceptions forcefully — but don't get drawn into a battle.

- **Snipers.** Snipers don't attack directly but take pot-shots from the sidelines. At meetings they may be whispering to others about you while you make a presentation. They are especially dangerous because they put on a facade of friendliness in front of their victims. To handle Snipers, Bramson suggests bringing the attack to the surface — for example: "That sounded like a dig. Did you mean it that way?" If the attack is made while you are making a presentation, bring it out on the spot: "Tom, by the way you're gesturing I get the idea you don't like what I'm proposing." You'll usually get a denial, but the sniping will stop — at least for the moment.

- **Negativists.** Negativists are down on every idea or suggestion made. Commonly heard from this type are such comments as "No, that will never work ..." or "We can't do that...." To cope with Negativists, you must remember that this type believes we are all victims of forces beyond our control. Bramson suggests making positive responses: "But when we tried this last year, management said it might be a good idea down the line." Or "This solution has worked for other departments." But whatever you say, don't argue. "Your strategy should be that some alternatives are worth trying even if the Negativist may be right that they won't work," Bramson contends.

Tip

The Team Grouch

Is there a grouch on your team? If so, you've probably discovered how difficult the grouch can be to work with. *Practical Supervision* offers these ideas for dealing with an irritating co-worker:

- **Don't overreact.** The grouch is looking for someone to irritate. Don't play along. Stay cool and detached.

- **Relax the tension.** Use a little humor. Joking in a non-malicious way can lighten everyone's spirits.

- **Undo the damage.** Team leaders can assign temperamental workers tasks to do on their own so they aren't able to stir up the others.

- **Make expectations clear.** Try to find out what's wrong. Team members should show empathy if there is a personal problem causing the behavior, but it should be clear that such moodiness must be kept out of the work group.

EXERCISE

ARE *YOU* A DIFFICULT PERSON?

Sometimes we are not fully aware of how we appear to others. Answer **YES** or **NO** to the following questions to help determine if others perceive you as difficult to work with:

1. Do you count to 10 before reacting when someone makes you angry? _____
2. Do you always try to smile and be pleasant? _____
3. Do you avoid overburdening others with your troubles? _____
4. Do you control stress through diet or exercise? _____
5. Do you give others the space they need when they're having a bad day? _____
6. Do you try to monitor your behavior when *you're* having a bad day? _____
7. Is it important to you to work well with others? _____
8. Are you someone *you* would like to work with? _____
9. Do you greet others by name? _____
10. Do you believe the secret to success in teamwork is getting along with others? _____

If you answered **YES** to at least eight questions, you've got a good grip on your gripes. Six or seven **YES** answers suggests you generally are easy to get along with, but people may not be sure what to expect on a given day. If you scored lower, you need to try harder to control your emotions.

Finding Common Ground When a Co-worker Doesn't Like You

You can employ strategies to resolve conflicts with teammates with whom you disagree on certain issues. And you can learn to handle teammates who are just difficult people. But what do you do when a teammate simply doesn't like *you*?

Well, you can try to ignore it, says management consultant Marilyn Moats Kennedy. Kennedy advises increasing contact with these teammates — for example, inviting them to lunch, joining them at breaks, or trying to engage them in chats before team meetings.

Why this approach? Kennedy says this forces your teammate to either warm up to you or to break down and admit there's a problem. If the teammate has made negative comments about you to others, you owe it to yourself to improve the relationship or at least determine what the problem is. By taking this assertive approach, you'll resolve the situation — one way or another.

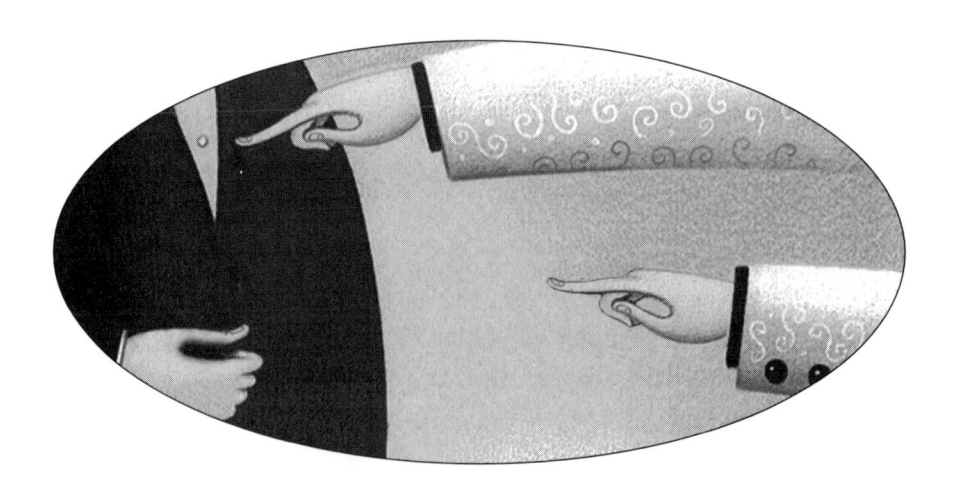

Resolving Arguments Among Team Members

Despite all efforts to peacefully resolve team conflicts, there may be times when full-fledged arguments erupt among team members. When you witness an altercation between teammates, here are a few strategies you can employ to help defuse the volatile situation:

- **Humor.** Chime in with a frivolous comment such as "End of round one!" or some other quip to help ease the tension. Chances are the parties don't realize how they appear to others, and this will give them a chance to laugh off the incident. But be prepared: There's also a chance they won't appreciate your joke — and will turn on you.

- **Rationality.** Arguments can quickly become irrational, shifting from issues to personalities. Try to get both parties to focus on the cause of the disagreement rather than attacking one another.

- **Camaraderie.** The bottom line is both parties are members of a team working together toward a common goal. Remind your dueling teammates of what they have in common. Try to help them see that they can accomplish more as allies than enemies.

- **Separation.** If an argument has gone far enough, it's possible no amount of reason will help. In this case, the best thing you and your fellow teammates can do is separate the parties until they have a chance to cool off.

Tip

My Regrets

It's always possible a teammate doesn't like you because *you've* done something to offend that person. What can you do when you've said something you regret?

- **Apologize immediately.** If you delay your apology, you leave time for bad feelings to mushroom.

- **Don't fan the flames.** If your transgression was so serious an apology isn't enough, don't aggravate the situation by continually bringing up the subject. Instead, make every effort to conduct yourself in such a way as to show that you didn't mean any harm. Actions speak louder than words. Give it some time.

- **Forgive yourself.** You can't turn back the clock and change what you've done. But you can learn from the experience. Do what you can to resolve the situation — and move on. And take the opportunity to learn to be forgiving of others who commit similar errors with you.

Learning to Laugh

Whether you're dealing with a difficult teammate or trying to resolve an issue-based conflict, humor can be a valuable tool for relieving stress — and improving productivity.

Humor "helps gain trust and makes others more receptive to your ideas," say Esther Blumenfeld and Lynne Alpern, authors of *The Smile Connection: How to Use Humor in Dealing with People* (Prentice Hall). They offer these suggestions for putting laughter and humor to work:

- **Don't be afraid to make a joke or funny remark when appropriate.** Listen to the remarks others make and judge for yourself what types of comments add to the moment. Get a feeling for what works in your team environment — and what doesn't. That doesn't mean imitating others, however. Find your own style.

- **If you don't get a laugh, let it go.** Don't take it personally. One reason we enjoy humor is that it is unpredictable and a little out of sync with the status quo. If you miss the mark once in a while, give yourself credit for trying.

- **Use humor for the right reasons.** Don't be the office clown or someone who wastes time by cracking jokes all day. Use humor to make others — and yourself — feel at ease and to build a comfortable relationship with teammates. You'll find that humor not only makes you laugh — it may help strengthen your team.

EXERCISE

HOW WELL DOES YOUR TEAM RESOLVE CONFLICT?

Does your team employ useful techniques and strategies when conflicts arise? Or do teammates allow conflict to disrupt meetings and undermine projects? Answer **YES** or **NO** to the following questions:

1. Do team members frequently disagree over insignificant issues? _____

2. When disagreements occur, do teammates focus more on personalities than issues? _____

3. Do team members try to shout over one another when making points? _____

4. Do team members refuse to compromise — even for the good of the project? _____

5. Are there teammates who refuse to work closely with one another? _____

6. During meetings, do opposing team members appear to line up on opposite sides of the room? _____

7. Have members of your team ever resorted to shouting and name-calling? _____

8. Do teammates avoid interacting outside team meetings? _____

9. Do some team members refuse to speak to others? _____

10. Are you a "team" in name only? _____

If you answered **YES** to *any* of these questions, your team may have a problem resolving conflict — a problem that could jeopardize the success of your project. Set aside a time to come together and clear the air, employing some of the conflict-resolution strategies provided in this chapter. If any team members refuse to participate, perhaps it's time to make personnel changes within the team.

conflict

What Would You Do?

A member of your work team seems to dislike you, and you hear from others that this member has made disparaging remarks about you. You've asked if something is wrong but were told, "Everything is fine." How do you approach the situation?

(Review "Finding Common Ground When a Co-worker Doesn't Like You" on page 96 for ideas.)

Team Activity

Does it seem like your teammates spend more time arguing than they spend in *positive* interaction? Try this team activity:

Initiate a roundtable discussion in which each team member in turn has to say something nice about a teammate. Continue until each team member has addressed every member of the group. If the team takes time to focus on members' good qualities, it will leave less time to focus on the negative.

CHAPTER 8
PROBLEM-SOLVING

If it were easy it would have been done before.
— **JEANNA YAEGER**
CO-PILOT OF ***VOYAGER,***
WHICH FLEW AROUND THE WORLD WITHOUT REFUELING

SEARCHING FOR SOLUTIONS

As production coordinator for a financial printer, Aldina Fuentes was responsible for keeping track of dozens of pamphlets and brochures and issuing a monthly report.

The problem? The company's accounting department changed its paperwork procedures weekly — frequently leaving Fuentes to redo reports to fit the new forms.

But rather than scream in frustration, Fuentes applied a problem-solving technique called "pairing." She met with representatives of the accounting department to give them a better understanding of how their work affected hers. Then they worked together to find a better way to handle the paperwork.

There's no magic formula for problem-solving. It's simply a matter of looking for creative alternatives to resolve dilemmas.

TIP
THREE STEPS TO PROBLEM-SOLVING

Clearer thinking and better problem-solving skills are not difficult to achieve. According to Dr. Edward de Bono, there are three easy steps to being a better problem-solver:

1. Quietly review the situation.

2. Generate alternatives. Consider all possible outcomes and forecast results.

3. Take your time. Don't rush — few situations in everyday life demand quick thinking or an immediate response. Look for the right answer, not the fast answer.

Brainstorming

One of the most popular — and successful — problem-solving techniques is brainstorming. Developed as a technique about 50 years ago, brainstorming has been adopted for many purposes such as generating new products, solving procedure problems, and establishing company policies.

Brainstorming entails little more than the free contribution of ideas to the group discussion. The facilitator's job is merely to introduce the problem and look to the team to offer solutions — the more the better.

One team member is designated to record it. Then the team is asked to toss out any idea that comes to mind — without worrying about how good or bad the idea may be.

Here are some guidelines for a successful brainstorming session:

- **Don't criticize or make value judgments.** Active participation is crucial to brainstorming. Each member should feel free to contribute to the session. Fear of rejection can only limit the number — and quality — of ideas offered.

- **Avoid taking credit.** Don't worry about recording *whose* idea it is. Some members may clam up if they feel they'll be held accountable if an idea is tried and fails.

- **Encourage free thinking.** The wilder the idea, the better. No one should be reluctant to voice what comes to mind. Encourage laughter and humor in the session. This can help fire imaginations — and lead to creative suggestions.

- **Keep ideas in full view.** Ideas should be recorded on a flip chart so they can be used as a springboard to other ideas.

Thinking Creatively

Have you ever wondered why some team members seem to come up with new and unusual approaches — solutions the rest of you have never considered?

In the book *A Whack on the Side of the Head* (Warner Books), author Roger von Oech offers the following suggestions for sparking creativity:

- **Don't always look for the right answer.** "We are taught to look for the one right answer," von Oech says. "Actually it's the second, third, or tenth right answer that solves the problem in an innovative way."

- **Don't always think logically.** Logic is appropriate when you're evaluating ideas. But when you're searching for ideas, logic can short-circuit creativity.

- **Avoid being too practical.** When faced with a problem, von Oech suggests, ask yourself "what if ..." and follow the thought down less practical paths than you might normally take.

- **Stop thinking you're not creative.** One of the major differences between creative people and noncreative people is that the former pay attention to their small ideas, knowing they could lead to a big breakthrough. "Believe in the worth of your ideas and have the persistence to build on them," von Oech advises.

Tip

The Dream Team

Sometimes the most far-fetched ideas are the ones that actually come to pass.

In the book *Risk and Other Four Letter Words* (Perennial Library), Walter B. Wriston points out that "the most accurate predictions of the future have come from science fiction writers and others with the courage to dream. Those who have relied on scientific research have almost always missed the mark."

Wriston notes that much of what author Jules Verne predicted 100 years ago has come to pass. On the other hand, a presidential commission appointed by Herbert Hoover in 1929 to forecast developments through 1952 "employed 500 researchers and failed even to mention atomic energy, jet propulsion, antibiotics, and many other significant developments."

The moral: Don't let so-called factual research deter your team from some creative risk-taking.

Take a Moment to ...

Get Your Creative Juices Flowing

Sometimes a new environment can do wonders for encouraging creative thinking. If your team is struggling with a seemingly unsolvable problem, make arrangements for the team to meet in a neutral setting that doesn't imply the same expectations as a conference room. How about a local restaurant, or a garden or picnic spot?

Once everyone is relaxed, have each person start throwing out ideas, following the brainstorming guidelines. Remember: Don't pre-judge any idea. Keep generating ideas for at least 15 minutes — preferably longer.

When you've run out of steam, go back over the ideas. Rule out the impossible and begin to discuss and refine what's left. You may find your "unsolvable" problem has a solution after all!

Exercise

Choose the Best Solution

Your team has done its brainstorming and come up with several viable options. Now, how do you turn options into solutions? You could try a couple of alternatives.

Divide the team into two groups, giving each a list of the alternatives. The first group will try the simple ranking method:

1. Discuss the problem and reach a consensus about what the solution should involve.

2. Eliminate any ideas that don't meet your agreed-upon objective.

3. Rank the remaining ideas according to how well they meet the objective.

The second group will try criteria-based ranking:

1. Again, discuss the problem and reach a consensus about what the solution should involve.

2. Determine the *criteria* the solution must meet in order to achieve that objective — for example: Will management likely accept it? Is it cost-effective? Can it be implemented in a timely manner?

3. Compare each proposed solution to the objective *and* the criteria. Give each proposal one point for meeting the objective and one point for meeting the criteria.

4. Add the scores. The proposal with the highest score would be the group's top choice.

Finally, bring both groups together and compare their choices. Did they reach the same conclusion?

Understanding Problems

Some problems that appear to be insurmountable are actually quite simple — and easily solved. Here are some of the common problems that plague teams and suggestions for resolving them:

1. The treadmill. Many teams waste valuable time and energy unnecessarily repeating tasks. In others, the proverbial right hand has no idea what the left is doing — and the result is duplicated effort. This problem can be eliminated by clearly outlining project goals and posting duty assignments so everyone is aware of who is doing what. Once an assignment is completed or a goal met, it should be noted on the assignment sheet.

2. The overrun. It doesn't matter how vital a project is if the team doesn't have the means to complete it. Teams should carefully budget each activity — and stick to the plan.

3. The bottleneck. When the pressure is on, it's easy for teams to get so caught up in the momentum that they scatter in all directions and lose focus. As a result, some projects are done haphazardly, while others are left undone. If your team is losing sight of its overall goal, take a moment before your next meeting to review the team mission statement. Look at the short-term goals you've devised to achieve your mission, and review the status of each project within that goal structure.

4. Unforeseen delays. Sometimes your team's projects can't be completed because other teams or vendors don't meet their obligations. When this occurs, don't just stand around waiting while your project suffers. Take action. If the other party can't resolve the situation, consider getting what you need from another source.

FINDING SOLUTIONS ... FAST!

What if a deadline is looming and there's no time to employ lengthy problem-solving techniques? There are different approaches for making group decisions quickly. Social scientists who study work teams have found a four-step process that brings out the creativity of team members rapidly — and usually generates a successful solution:

1. List ideas. The team should allot about 20 minutes for each member to compile a list of possible solutions to the problem. This technique is similar to brainstorming, but because of time constraints contributors should be more discriminating, focusing on ideas that are immediately doable. The team must come up with an action plan without benefit of a lot of research and debate. Experience and professional instinct must be relied upon to find a quick solution.

2. Create a master list. In round-robin fashion, each team member gives the team leader one idea. The idea is recorded on a flip chart for everyone to see. The process continues until each member's list is exhausted.

3. Clarify ideas. Team members are then given the opportunity to clarify any ideas on the master list. This is not an invitation to discussion but an opportunity to any answer questions members may have about specific proposals.

4. Cast secret votes. Finally, members are asked to vote on paper for the idea they like best. The votes are tallied and the least popular ideas eliminated. Then the top vote-getters are reviewed by the group — with as little discussion as possible — until a consensus is reached.

Take a Moment to ...

Get Unstuck

Your work team is struggling with a problem. You're stumped, and you need a creative approach to finding new answers. Try these ideas:

- **Slow down!** Take a deep breath and give yourselves a little space. You're less likely to make a mistake if you don't rush a decision.

- **Don't limit alternatives.** Open your minds to as many different possibilities as you can. Don't dismiss an idea because it's different. Give it time and look at it from different angles.

- **Don't look back.** Put the old ways aside and look for a new approach.

- **Write it down.** Putting thoughts on paper jogs memory, which can help you move in new directions and explore uncharted territory.

Calling In an Expert

If problems were *easy* to solve, it wouldn't take a team to do it. And it's not unusual for even a team to get in too deep — to a point where the information is too technical or complex for most members to comprehend.

When this happens, team members may be embarrassed to admit they don't grasp key facts or concepts. Worse, more stubborn members may try to forge ahead, attempting to tackle something they don't understand.

When it becomes obvious people are getting confused or that the conversation is going in circles, it's time to bring in an expert. Team members should realize that it's OK not to be familiar with every facet of the project, and it's better to get accurate information than to waste time continuing without it. It never hurts to get another point of view.

Exercise

Improving Skills in Problem-Solving

This quiz can help you find the strengths and weaknesses of your problem-solving skills, as well as point you to ways of improving in this important area. Answer **YES** or **NO**:

1. Do you gather all the relevant information you can before trying to solve a problem? _____
2. Do you seek input from your teammates? _____
3. Do you get opinions from outside experts? _____
4. Do you list all the possible solutions on a piece of paper? _____
5. Do you then visualize the strengths and weaknesses of each solution? _____
6. Do you let your subconscious work on the problem? _____
7. Do others seek your help? _____
8. Are you willing to try another solution if your first idea isn't working? _____
9. Do you see problems as challenges and get satisfaction from resolving them? _____
10. Do you practice your problem-solving skills on puzzles and games? _____

Eight or more **YES** answers indicates you are a pro at solving problems. Six or seven is average, but if you had a lower score, study the questions for ways to improve.

What Would You Do?

Your team is in over its head. In analyzing a problem, the group has reached the point where information is too technical and abstract to be understood. Members are lost and discouraged. How would you get the team moving again?

(Review "Calling In an Expert" on page 114 for ideas.)

Team Activity

Does your team have trouble choosing between alternative proposals? Try this decision-making activity:

Select one member of your team to champion each of the positions in question. Avoid choosing people who already strongly favor one position; instead, look for neutral people who can build an objective case. Ask each person to prepare a short presentation on the merits of the position. Then ask the team to vote. This can help you make a quick and democratic decision.

MAKE YOUR TEAM A WINNER!

CHAPTER 9

A TEAM MEMBER'S GUIDE TO PERSONAL DEVELOPMENT AND WELL-BEING

Strive for excellence in everything you do and you will assure yourself of satisfaction.
— MARTHA LAYNE COLLINS

FINDING SUCCESS

Being part of a team is a collective activity. But that doesn't mean you should neglect the individual. Teams are only as strong as their members. If members are experiencing stress, suffering from burnout, or poorly managing their projects, it can affect the team as a whole. So, it's important for team members to nurture themselves while they're focused on the common goal.

What does it take to achieve personal success? A few years ago, Robert A. Beck, chairman emeritus of Prudential, shared his thoughts during a Wall Street seminar:

- **Beat yesterday.** "Always produce more than you did the day before."

- **Success is never an accident.** "Every good record is built with defined goals and a realistic strategy. It doesn't just happen."

- **Be a good example.** "You don't have to be an extrovert, but you should look like a positive force in the way you walk, dress, and meet colleagues."

- **Get involved.** "Reach out for new opportunities; be involved in industry matters, not just in your own company."

- **Make your career fun.** "Once you master a task you don't like, it's easier and also a source of pride and accomplishment."

- **Let the music out.** "Too many people live and die with the music still in them. Be fully committed; then you will achieve your goals."

- **Success is easier than failure.** "Working hard is not difficult as long as you are getting the results you want. It's easier to live with yourself when you can be proud of what you've done."

Another key factor in determining success is your ability to skillfully converse with the teammates and managers who will have an impact on the course of your career. The first rule of the clever conversationalist is never underestimate the value of small talk.

In her book *Letitia Baldrige's Complete Guide to Executive Manners* (Macmillan), Letitia Baldrige describes a good conversationalist as:

- **Well-informed.** No matter what business you are in, you should be prepared to participate, to at least a small degree, in discussions about such subjects as art, politics, and science.

- **Able to quickly change directions.** Being able to move easily from one subject to another is seen as a sign of intelligence.

- **Looking others in the eye.** "Eye contact is very important," Baldrige writes. Failing to look at others when you're speaking could signal you are embarrassed, frightened, or hiding something.

- **Hesitant to interrupt.** "It is extremely rude to interrupt someone," Baldrige says, "even if that person is dragging on interminably."

- **Knowing how to query without prying.** New people will be flattered by interest, but Baldrige advises keeping that interest general. It's one thing to ask what people do for a living — it's another to ask their salary.

Of course, the opposite of being a good conversationalist is being a bore — something you'd want to avoid.

Researchers at the University of Chicago asked students to rate 43 boring behaviors. Here are the top eight ways to ensure that no one will want to talk with you:

- Complaining about your problems and not being interested in the problems of others.
- Talking constantly about trivial things and repeating old jokes.
- Showing no emotion, talking in a monotone, and failing to make eye contact.
- Being too serious.
- Being tedious and talking too slowly.
- Never joining in a conversation, just going along with whatever is said.
- Being distracting by overusing such expressions as "you know."
- Being self-centered — always talking about your life and interests.

Take a Moment to ...

Fine-Tune Your Conversation Skills

If you're not sure what makes a good conversationalist, think about your teammates. Is there someone you'd describe as a good conversationalist, someone you particularly enjoy talking to? Try to find an opportunity to observe this individual speaking to others. At your first opportunity, jot down those qualities that seem to make this individual's discourse more interesting than that of other teammates. Can you adopt any of these techniques to improve your conversation skills?

Now, is there anyone on the team you find boring? Jot down the qualities that make you want to avoid conversing with this person. Be honest. Do you display any of these qualities?

> **TIP**
>
> ## OFFICE LANGUAGE
>
> Are you an interesting person or a bore? The answer won't be found solely in what you say — your office or workstation can also speak volumes.
>
> If your office is a sterile place that makes visitors relive childhood visits to the principal, consider the following ideas to make your work space more accessible to others:
>
> - Add a few personal mementos or books to give clues about your values and interests.
>
> - Exhibit some family photos or children's drawings that can help others see you have a life outside the office.
>
> - Display relevant certificates and diplomas to demonstrate your expertise — and include any awards that can emphasize your belief in excellence.

STAYING CHALLENGED

Another way to achieve success is to strive to be continually challenged in your projects. In their book *The Achievement Challenge* (Dow Jones-Irwin), Don Beveridge and Jeffrey P. Davidson offer these tips:

1. Hone your skills. "It doesn't matter what you produced last year ... the challenge is to improve."

2. Sweat! "Physically being in the work environment is not a standard in itself. Productivity is the real key."

3. Be yourself. "The challenge in achieving, excelling, and getting ahead ... is to use the best of your abilities, skills, and style."

4. Maintain your integrity. "... Ethics, business morals, and integrity are uncompromising standards."

5. Innovate. "How can I do a job better? What new ideas can I implement?"

MANAGING TIME

One of the biggest challenges workers face is learning to successfully manage the clock. Often team members are torn between regular job duties and team responsibilities — and personal well-being gets lost along the way.

In the book *Careertracking* (Simon & Schuster), authors Jimmy Calano and Jeff Shalzman offer the following suggestions for making time more productive:

1. **Plan tomorrow's workday today.** List your objectives and rank them by priority. Also estimate the amount of time each activity should take.

2. **Know your daily high and low points.** Do you hit your stride in the morning or afternoon? Don't fight your personal rhythms. Whenever possible, schedule routine tasks and appointments for low-energy periods and important duties for when you're most alert.

3. **Deal with the worst first.** Get the most unpleasant people and most dreaded assignments out of the way first, and you'll create momentum that can carry you through the rest of your day.

4. **Use visualization skills.** During your morning commute, visualize that you are actually heading home, feeling good for having completed everything just as you'd planned. The authors say this exercise can make your day seem less intimidating by creating a mental program you'll unconsciously follow to a successful conclusion.

But even the best-laid plans sometimes fail. The culprit: time robbers — those little interruptions that can throw your entire schedule off course.

In an article in *USA Today* magazine, business professor Barbara Chrispin said people have control of only 25 percent of their workday — the rest is taken up by unexpected activities. "These activities are not exactly wasteful but cut into time that could be spent on other things," she says.

Here are some common time robbers — and suggestions for thwarting them:

- **Telephone calls.** When possible, rely on receptionists or voice mail to field telephone calls; then set a designated time for returning calls.

- **Visitors.** When unexpected visitors approach, be polite but keep paperwork in your hands to convey the sense that you're busy. Mention that you're working to meet a deadline and suggest an alternative time to meet.
- **Reading and mail.** Set aside a specific time to go through your mail and read any time-sensitive material. If someone wants your opinion on a report, make your notes directly on the cover page or a large Post-it™ note as you read — then return the item immediately. Never let paperwork go through your hands twice.
- **Poor delegating.** Where appropriate, delegate to others matters that don't require your personal touch.

TIP

DOUBLE DUTY

Sometimes team members have difficulty managing their time because no one could handle the number of obligations they carry. Good performers are often overworked because others believe they can get the job done. So what do you do if you've become the team's Super Member?

In her book *Games Mother Never Taught You* (Rawson Associates), Betty Lehan Harragan says you should address the problem directly. Review your team assignments with the team leader. Explain that — while you're flattered by the vote of confidence — you can't live up to expectations while juggling so many projects. And stress that stretching yourself too thin will only hurt the team in the long run. It's a *team* effort — don't be afraid to ask for help.

Of course, for some people the real culprit in learning to manage time effectively isn't an unwelcome visitor or over-demanding team leader — it's the face in the mirror, otherwise known as the *procrastinator.*

If procrastination is your problem, try the following:

1. Time yourself. Procrastinators are often unrealistic in estimating how long projects will take. Begin timing how long it takes you to complete regular tasks and you'll know how much time to allot in the future.

2. Start on time. Procrastinators often get a late start and then forever play catch-up. Set a time to begin each project — and stick to it.

3. Break projects down. Sometimes procrastinators are hesitant to get going when a project seems overwhelming. Rather than looking at a project as a huge undertaking, break it down into a series of small, easily achievable tasks.

4. Expect interruptions. Interrupt a procrastinator and the whole day lost. Plan time in your schedule for a certain number of interruptions, and don't let them keep you from coming back to your work.

5. Use your energy wisely. Whether it's mid-morning or late afternoon, tackle demanding projects during your most productive time.

> **TIP**
>
> ## TIME MISSPENT
>
> Unfortunately, no matter how diligent people are at managing their time, some time is still lost to pointless pursuits. Priority Management Pittsburgh, Inc., a consulting firm, studied hundreds of people for over a year to determine how they spent their time. According to company president Michael Fortino:
>
> - Most people spend five years waiting in line and six months trapped at traffic lights.
>
> - The average person spends one year searching for misplaced objects and four years doing housework.
>
> - People spend eight months opening junk mail and two years trying to return phone calls to people who never seem to be in.
>
> To make some of this time a little more productive, Fortino suggests planning travel routes around radio traffic reports and passing the time while waiting in line by reading or planning.

TAKE A MOMENT TO ...

CLEAN YOUR DESK

It's difficult to dive into a new day's project when the previous day's junk is in the way. But, you say, cleaning your desk could take half the morning. Not necessarily.

To clean your desk in two minutes, follow these tips suggested by *Writer's Digest:*

1. Stack everything on your desk in one pile — paper, books, pencils ... everything. Don't think, just stack.

2. Move the stack to the floor next to your trash can.

3. Sort through the stack and put everything into two piles: one to act on now, the other to file. Throw the rest away.

When you reach the point in your day's schedule for doing paperwork, your goal is to handle each piece in the remaining piles only once. When in doubt, throw it away. Don't procrastinate — decide then and there.

clean

EXERCISE

You Can Be More Organized!

If you're disorganized, don't despair. Some of the most organized people in the world were once among the most disorganized. This quiz is intended to help you see your organizing strengths and weaknesses. Answer **YES** or **NO**:

1. When meeting with your team, do you always come prepared? _____
2. Do you sort your work into piles by priority? _____
3. At the end of the day do you make a list of your next day's priorities? _____
4. Do you list recommended actions? _____
5. Do you start each day by tackling your most immediate goals? _____
6. Do you spot-check yourself to be sure you're staying on schedule? _____
7. Do you congratulate yourself when you complete a task? _____
8. Do you allow time for the unexpected such as phone calls and interruptions? _____
9. Do you check items off your list as you accomplish them? _____
10. Do you help keep team meetings organized and on schedule? _____

Seven or more **YES** answers is a sign you are organized. If you scored lower, go to the library and check out a book on getting organized to find suggestions for improving.

Managing Stress

One of the greatest obstacles to developing personal well-being in a team environment — or any work environment — is stress. Today stress is blamed for everything from violence in the workplace to life-threatening illness. But there are techniques that can help you cope with job-related stress. Try the following stress-reducing ideas:

- Get up 15 minutes earlier to avoid feeling rushed and tense on your morning commute.
- Prepare for each morning the night before. By deciding what you'll wear and making sure your keys and briefcase are by the door, you'll save a lot of last-minute headaches in the morning.
- Make duplicates of all keys. There's nothing to get a day off to a bad start like losing the keys to your car or office.
- Make a copy of your appointment book every week or so. For some people, life without a day planner is ... unmanageable. Accidents happen, so be prepared.
- Take advantage of off hours for banking and shopping. Try to miss the crowds by avoiding peak times like Friday evenings.
- Don't put up with anything that doesn't work properly. Machines are there help you — not to cause you stress. If it doesn't work, get it fixed or replace it.
- Unclutter your life. Get rid of things you never use.

TIP

TUNE OUT

Rather than letting your morning commute be a cause for additional stress, use the time to decompress. Avoid loud music, depressing news stories, or sniping shock jocks. Instead, opt for some soft music ... or just silence. Tuning out while driving in can help you brace for the chaos of the day.

When it comes to living a healthier, more stress-free lifestyle, little things can add up to a lot. Take these steps to improve your overall health:

- **Stretch in bed.** Take a few extra minutes to ease into the day.
- **Eat a good breakfast.** Replenish your depleted energy reserves.
- **Limit caffeine.** Large amounts of caffeine can cause insomnia, trembling, and headaches.
- **Eat a healthful snack.** Try to avoid those mid-morning doughnuts. Opt instead for a piece of fruit.
- **Eat a healthful lunch.** Include some protein to get you over that afternoon slump.
- **Drink more water.** Water aids kidney and liver functions and helps maintain body temperature.
- **Take a walk.** A 20-minute walk each day is an easy way to promote cardiovascular fitness.

Tip

Weekend Respite

According to a nationwide survey done for Hilton Hotels, most Americans spend 14 hours each weekend doing chores, running errands, and meeting other obligations. Eighty-four percent of those surveyed said they feel no more energetic at the end of a weekend than at the end of a hectic work week.

Try breaking your chores into smaller parts and doing as many as possible during the week. Save the weekend for more pleasurable — and relaxing — activities.

Take a Moment to ...

Exercise While You Work

Exercising is a great way to beat stress and increase energy, but it's difficult to get the exercise you need while sitting at your desk. Still, you can make the office more fitness friendly by incorporating the following activities into your workday:

- **Take the stairs.** If you can't make the nine flights to your desk, fine — take the elevator to the eighth floor and walk the rest of the way.
- **Do a few push-ups or deep-knee bends.** If you can't push up from the floor, try using your desk to position yourself at a 45-degree angle and go from there.
- **Take a lunchtime walk.** Even 10 minutes of walking can help relieve stress and improve fitness.
- **Hold in that gut.** Sit up straight at your desk, pull in your stomach, tighten the muscles, and hold for a count of five. Repeat several times.
- **Don't slump.** To avoid low-back problems, try to maintain proper posture — especially when working at the computer.

TIP

REST YOUR EYES

If you've been doing close work, like writing or reading, for a long period of time, give your eyes a 60-second break. Gaze off into the distance, focusing on the horizon. Let your eyes rest there for a full minute to help keep your eyes from "locking up."

Exercise

Check Your Health

Take the following quiz to determine whether you are doing the right things to maintain your health — and your contribution to your team. Answer **YES** or **NO**:

1. Do you exercise regularly? _____
2. Do you get all the sleep you need? _____
3. Do you try to avoid overeating? _____
4. Do you avoid junk foods? _____
5. Do you avoid nicotine — in all forms? _____
6. Do you take time to relax? _____
7. Do you control your caffeine intake? _____
8. Do you keep your alcohol intake low? _____
9. Do you take periodic vacations and weekend trips? _____
10. Do you take care of your mental health by maintaining a bright outlook? _____

Eight or more **YES** answers is a sign that you're taking control of your health. Keep up the good work! Regardless of your score, work on changing those **NO** answers to **YES**.

Making the Most of a Bad Day

You may not feel continually stressed, but even the most easygoing people have bad days. And when you're having one of *those* days, there are things you can do to make it bearable.

"People have a bad day when they feel out of control," says Bruce A. Baldwin in *It's All in Your Head: Lifestyle Management Strategies for Busy People* (Direction Dynamics). "They feel like they are victims of events."

One way to fight that feeling is to take on a project that can restore your sense of control. Tackle an assignment you know won't be a problem. Organize a file, rearrange bookshelves — anything that will give you a feeling of control over your environment. Here are some additional suggestions:

- Allow yourself a mini-indulgence.
- Plan lunch with a friend.
- Vent to a trusted confidant.
- Engage in some physical activity to lift your spirits.

Another way to overcome a bad day is to turn to the tried and true: laughter.

William Fry, professor of clinical psychiatry at Stanford University, has studied laughter for 30 years. He told *USA Today* magazine that laughing 100 times a day is approximately equivalent to 10 minutes of exercise on a rowing machine. Fry has found that laughter can strengthen the immune system, improve breathing, and lessen perceptions of pain.

Rather than being trivial and inconsequential, Fry describes laughter as "vital in terms of health and interactions."

BATTLING BURNOUT

What if, however, the problem is not a bad day but something more serious — burnout. Teams working on a difficult project over a long period often experience burnout — either as a group or individually.

In their book *Take This Job and Love It* (Fireside Books), Dennis Jaffe and Cynthia D. Scott name six key skills you need to break the grip of job burnout:

1. Take care of your physical well-being.

2. Respond directly to difficulties and demands rather than avoiding them.

3. Utilize the help and support of other people.

4. Focus energy on mastering some part of a challenge rather than trying to do it all.

5. Take time out to rethink your approach when things are not working out.

6. Try to manage your time more effectively.

CELEBRATING SUCCESS

Another way to avoid burnout is to take time to celebrate your success. Whether you've achieved your long-term mission, or have just knocked off the first of your short-term goals, it's important for you and your teammates to take time to applaud your own efforts. After all, if you don't appreciate yourselves, you can't expect others to appreciate you.

TAKE A MOMENT TO ...

HAVE A PARTY

Your team doesn't have to accomplish something spectacular to have reason to celebrate. Just getting a group of people to work together to achieve a common goal is enough reason for kudos.

To give everyone in the group something to look forward to, plan a monthly or bimonthly party. It doesn't have to be an elaborate affair — you could settle for a happy-hour mixer. Just remember: It's a celebration. Avoid discussing any negatives about your project. Stay focused on the positive things you've accomplished together.

Exercise

Do You Have a Winning Attitude?

A winning attitude should be one of your chief goals in personal development. This quiz can help you judge for yourself whether you've developed this necessary trait. Answer **YES** or **NO** to the following questions:

1. Do you learn from your mistakes? _____
2. Do you set goals for yourself? _____
3. Are you able to examine problems from unique perspectives? _____
4. Do you enjoy the challenges of your job? _____
5. Do you take pride in your work? _____
6. If you disagree with a member of your team, do you make known your viewpoint in a positive way? _____
7. Do you ask questions? _____
8. Do you think others feel comfortable asking you questions? _____
9. Do you enjoy looking for novel solutions to problems? _____
10. Do you have a healthy attitude about your team and teammates? _____

Eight or more **YES** answers means you probably have a winning attitude on the job and off. If you scored lower, you may be guilty of negativism. Try to focus on the positive and you'll be more successful in your work and personal life.

What Would You Do?

There was a time when you enjoyed your team activities. Now you barely make it through the workday and are beginning to resent the intrusion of the team on your time. How can you go about reenergizing yourself?

(Review "Double Duty" on page 125 for ideas.)

Team Activity

Do your teammates need to take more time to relax? Try this activity based on recommendations by Joan Borysenko in *Minding the Body, Mending the Mind* (Addison-Wesley):

Have everyone in the group find a comfortable sitting position. Ask all members to breathe deeply, relaxing their muscles one at a time, starting with their heads and moving gradually down to their toes. Have them silently pick a word to focus on —any phrase that means something to them — and repeat it silently in time with their breathing. Do this for five minutes.

Conclusion

In this book, we've looked at how to be better team members, team leaders, conflict resolvers, problem solvers — and happier and healthier people.

Some of the exercises focused on team activities — others on the individuals within the team. Some required a lot of thought. Others were offered in a spirit of fun. All were intended to help you think more like a team player — to encourage you to offer greater support to your teammates and to help you gain greater support from them.

Teamwork is serious business, so it's doubtful your team will have time to engage in all the spirited "Team Activities" suggested at the end of each chapter. But working some of these activities into your schedule may encourage your team to become a stronger unit. And that can only help you achieve your mission — and make your team a winner!

Complete Your Teamwork Library with These Dartnell Books and Audiotapes

How to Make Teamwork WORK:
Targeting Team Members' Roles to Get the Best Results

Teamwork is still difficult and elusive for many people. Your employees may feel confused, frightened, or fascinated by the team process — and this workbook is an excellent guide for all of them. Five 20-minute sessions are offered including the following team-building skills:
- Defining Roles and Responsibilities
- Recipe for Team Success
- Working Together: The Team Process

96-page workbook; paperback; $12.95
Product code: 8145

Problem-Solving Techniques for Teams

Whether they're still wet behind the ears or have been around the block a few times, all teams face problems. This workbook will help your team members discover problem-solving secrets that they can put to use again and again. It offers five 20-minute sessions on:
- Identifying Problems
- Generating Solutions
- Choosing and Implementing Solutions
- Solving Team Problems
- Solving Ethical Problems

88-page workbook; paperback; $12.95
Product code: 8146

Attitude and Action: Building Winning Teams at Work and at Home

In this inspiring and powerful audio program, Mike Singletary, former Defense Team Captain for the Chicago Bears, explains:
- How to create lasting success by consistently refocusing and setting new goals
- How to become a self-motivated and enthusiastic team player able to remain committed to the purpose
- What it takes to win!

1 audiocassette;
running time: approximately 1 hour;
$10.95; Product code: 2079

The Communication Connection
How to Get Your Message Across Verbally and Nonverbally

Get rid of communication problems once and for all. In five 20-minute sessions, you'll learn how to interact more effectively with co-workers, customers, and your boss ... how to improve your writing skills ... how to make the most of communication technologies ... and much more. This workbook will teach you:
- How to "criticize with care"
- 10 ways to write more clearly
- How to use non-verbal communication
- Ways to handle face-to-face conflicts

96-page workbook; paperback; $12.95
Product code: 8177

Quick Quizzes
133 Ways to Measure Success

This fun, interactive training tool makes the monitoring and measuring of employee progress easy by providing short, self-explanatory quizzes designed for use by supervisors, managers, and trainers in a workplace setting. The quizzes cover important areas of business relations, such as customer service, teamwork, sales, self-development, and interpersonal skills, and can be used in a group setting such as in a meeting, or on an individual basis.

168 pages; paperback; $12.95
Product code: 1339

Get additional copies of
Make Your Team a Winner!
for every member of your team. Elevate your team to an even higher level tomorrow by ordering today!

YES, send me the following product(s) in the quantities I have indicated. I understand that if I am not completely satisfied, I may return the product(s) within 30 days for a full refund.

_____ ***Make Your Team a Winner!***; $12.95; Product code: 8550

_____ ***How to Make Teamwork WORK***; $12.95; Product code: 8145

_____ ***Problem-Solving Techniques for Teams***; $12.95; Product code: 8146

_____ ***Attitude and Action***; $10.95; Product code: 2079

_____ ***The Communication Connection***; $12.95; Product code: 8177

_____ ***Quick Quizzes***; $12.95; Product code: 1339

(Plus shipping & handling. IL residents please add 8.75% tax, Canada 7% GST. Prices subject to change.)

Bill my: ❏ VISA   ❏ American Express   ❏ MasterCard   ❏ Company

Card Number _____ Exp. Date _____

Signature _____

Name _____ Title _____

Company _____

Address _____

City/State/ZIP _____

Phone ( ) _____ Fax ( ) _____

(Signature and phone number are necessary to process order.)

❏ Please send me your latest catalog.   ❏ Please call to tell me about quantity discounts.

Copies may be ordered from your bookseller or from Dartnell. To order from Dartnell, call toll-free (800) 621-5463, or fax us your order (800) 327-8635 or visit our Web site at www.dartnellcorp.com

DARTNELL
4660 N RAVENSWOOD AVE, CHICAGO, IL 60640-4595